# SCREWED

# SCREWED

## Dancing with the Generals

From Ceausescu's Romania to Obama's America:
Reflections and recollections of an Associated Press reporter
from forty years in Europe and the United States

Sergiu Viorel Urma

ISBN: 0692413502
ISBN 13: 9780692413500
Library of Congress Control Number: 2015940814
Sergiu Viorel Urma, Cliffside Park, NJ

*To Carmen, my rock*

"Socialism is the same as Communism, only better English."

_ G. B. SHAW

*Urma Sergiu Viorel "is engaged in gathering and transmitting abroad data with a tendentious and disparaging content about our country through the intermediary of the 'Associated Press' agency and 'Radio Free Europe.'"*

—ROMANIAN *SECURITATE* DOSSIER NO. 223442

# Prelude

After a twenty-three-year break, during which the Associated Press did not have a reporter in communist Romania, the agency opened a Bucharest bureau in 1973, naming Nick Ludington as its head correspondent. I became his assistant for a year until 1974 when he moved to Beirut, after being promoted to Chief of Middle East Services.

The United States and the West were curious to know if Romania was really the "crack" in the Soviet bloc that seemed to have been created after the crushing of the Prague Spring in 1968, or if everything was a mere deception. Was Ceausescu a "maverick leader," independent of Moscow and open to the West, or was he fooling around? Was he a Trojan horse or a totalitarian bully?

After I became the AP's sole hand in the country, a cat-and-mouse game would start between me—the only independent Romanian hired and paid by a Western news medium in Ceausescu's Romania—and the political police known as the *Securitate*, which tortured and humiliated Leonard Kirschen so much. As Romania's economic situation progressively worsened, I came into open conflict with the authorities, who worked hard to "document my activity of treason" and remove me from my job.

Before joining AP, I often asked myself what the incentives were to "succeed" in a totalitarian system: The ambition to control other people and be feared by them? The belief that you're smarter and deserve better? The "art" of survival? Soon I would find out the answer to this question.

For me, it was the illusion of freedom: to be able to feel free even if I was watched day and night and to avoid sinking into the cesspit many deliberately chose in order to curry favor with the regime and enjoy the advantages. It was my chance, and I didn't have any merits apart from the fact that I didn't care much about the price I'd have to pay. Sometimes, I admit, I was fearful of the consequences, but I never looked back.

*Viorel Urma is in the attention of Service 1 being suspected of spying for the United States of America.*

—DOSSIER NOTE SIGNED BY SENIOR LIEUTENANT
MURESAN P., SEPTEMBER 11, 1980

Bucharest
Spring 2014

Old habits die hard.

I am in the reading room at the National Council for the Study of the Securitate Archives, the authority that administers the archives of the former communist political police in Romania. In front of me lies Dossier No. 223442, put together by the feared Securitate, Romania's version of the Soviet KGB. The bulky folder has several hundred handwritten and typed pages. All of them mention in the upper right-hand corner *STRICT SECRET, exemplar unic.*

In addition to these pages, there is another file on microfilm, since the "blue-eyed boys" (so called because of the light-blue color of the epaulettes on their Securitate formal uniforms) worked hard to discredit and remove me from the Associated Press bureau in Bucharest.

It took me nine years to get access to my secret police files. When I first applied for the right to see the contents of my binder in 2005, I was told that Romania's new, pro-Western authorities would need time to look in the vast archive that contains more than one hundred million pages, or five pages per each Romanian on average. If laid end to end, the paper would stretch twelve and a half miles.

I am reading from the dossier, and I can't believe my eyes: they suspected me of engaging in espionage, but, honestly, I wasn't aware of doing this. Was I a spy without knowing it? Was I working while sleepwalking? I could imagine saying, "Sure, thanks for the information, but I don't believe I am guilty of anything."

"It doesn't matter, Mr. Urma. *We* know better than you do! You'd better confess if you don't want us to make you 'walk' barefoot to Brasov like your former AP colleague, what's his name…Kirschen…the Romanian Jew who spent ten years in the lockup."

I have no idea who this Senior Lieutenant Muresan P. is. (May he rest in peace if he kicked the bucket by now.) But his report was attached to my dossier after a meeting of the foreign press with officials of the Department of Cults in 1980 where the topic of "religious freedom" in Romania was discussed—as well as some "ill-meaning news reports that slandered the realities" in our beloved homeland.

I had asked a question about the Baptist Church. At the time it was experiencing some problems with the communist authorities, such as a lack of pastors and churches for the growing number of Baptist believers. At the end of our discussion, a youthful-looking man from their entourage asked me if I wanted to subscribe to the monthly magazine published by the state-run Department of Cults. I said yes, why not, and we chatted amicably for several minutes, and that was all.

In the handwritten dossier note, the baby-faced cults tipster—who didn't introduce himself by name—reported our conversation to his Securitate handler, and at the bottom of the page, Muresan P. attached his own observation to justify his existence and salary. They suspected me of spying for the United States! I couldn't believe they were so thick thirty years after the communist takeover. It's the only reference in my dossier to my "espionage" activity, and I believe that Senior Lieutenant Muresan P. wanted to impress his superiors with his range of knowledge. I had little doubt that he was a brainwashed blockhead like so many others working in his field.

The Department of Cults was swarming with undercover agents keeping under surveillance the Romanian Orthodox Church and the other religious denominations, and reporting on the clerics' movements and

discussions. Even among the clergy, there were informers and collaborators—paid or unpaid—whose mission was less divine and more mundane:
uncover and isolate the "enemies" of the regime. One of the stated missions of the Department of State Security (DSS) was the "particular attention for actions under religious cover" to infiltrate the "neo-Protestant
sects and the Greek Catholic cult" in Transylvania and other parts of the
country. Their aim was to "get information about and annihilate the foreign envoys of cultic centers" in Romania. Among them were "illegal religious groups" such as Jehovah's Witnesses and Seventh-day Adventists.

These activities were the responsibility of the 1$^{st}$ Directorate of
Internal Security, the 3$^{rd}$ Directorate of Counterespionage, and the Service
"D" (Disinformation). Fine, but what was the connection between me and
these cultic centers that had to be deactivated? From what I read in my
dossier, I concluded that they wanted to deactivate me.

Ceausescu's counterintelligence watched me closely. My name was in-
cluded in all the written notes coming to and leaving from the 3$^{rd}$ Directorate
in the DSS and carrying the names of illustrious generals, such as Gheorghe
Zagoneanu, deputy chief of CIE (Center of External Intelligence) after
September 1978 (following the defection to the United States of General
Ion Mihai Pacepa); Stefan Alexie, head of the 3$^{rd}$ Directorate after 1982;
Aurelian Mortoiu, former chief of counterintelligence; and Iulian Vlad,
deputy minister of internal affairs, which was in charge of the secret police
known as the Securitate and the regular police force.

I did not know I was such an important person, seriously.

In front of me, there is a report labeled "strict secret" dealing with the
closing of the individual surveillance dossier the Securitate was working
on in my case for some time. The file, known by its Romanian acronym
*DUI* (Dossier of Informative Surveillance), was described as a "superior
form of monitoring," probably to distinguish it from the general intelligence surveillance that all Romanians were blessed with by the communist regime. Actually, it was the most comprehensive type of secret
police surveillance and the *DUI* was meant to later serve in the person's
arrest and imprisonment. The decision to close it was taken after the authorities took note of the protests by AP's management and the US State

Department. This decision is on page 313 of Dossier 223442, and dated January 19, 1986. This is what it says verbatim, in the wooden language used by the authorities:

*On February 26, 1985, an individual surveillance dossier was opened in the case of Romanian citizen URMA SERGIU VIOREL, born on [...] in Bucharest, a technical-administrative worker of the American agency "Associated Press" in Bucharest, for the following suspicions:*

*—he has dubious relations with diplomats accredited to Bucharest and with other foreign citizens visiting our country*

*—he is involved in gathering and transmitting abroad data with a tendentious and disparaging content about our country through the intermediary of the "Associated Press" agency and the "Free Europe" radio station.*

*For documenting and halting the hostile activity unfolded by URMA SERGIU VIOREL, in the process of evidence gathering we used our sources "CORNEL" and "ANDREI," and special measures were carried out at the home of the objective [i.e., URMA], as well as the office of the "Associated Press" agency where he unfolds his professional activity. The following facts have been established:*

*It was confirmed that URMA SERGIU VIOREL, despite the fact that he is not accredited as a correspondent of American agency "Associated Press," was engaged in recent years in writing and publishing abroad a series of materials meant to create an unfavorable image for our country. Noteworthy in this regard are his articles about the Decree no. 93/1983 regarding the regime of multiplication/photocopy machines (and) of... typewriters, as well as those referring to the "lawbreaking phenomenon in the RS Romania" (transmitted periodically) and some "problems" facing our society, presented in a tendentious and disparaging way in the foreign press.*

*URMA SERGIU VIOREL contacted Father CALCIU GHEORGHE immediately after he was released from imprisonment and interviewed him for a biased story he wrote for and sent to the "Associated*

*Press" agency through which he wanted to present [CALCIU] as a victim of the regime. The articles transmitted by URMA SERGIU VIOREL were picked up and circulated by several foreign publications, as well as the "Free Europe" radio station, which led to the launching of some hostile actions by the Western media.*

*To counteract the hostile activity unfolded by URMA SERGIU VIOREL, with the approval of the management of the Department of State Security, in September 1985 [URMA] was warned by the Ministry of Foreign Affairs.*

*In this regard, URMA SERGIU VIOREL was summoned to MFA's Department of Press and Culture and informed that because he is not accredited as a correspondent of the "Associated Press" agency he went beyond his ordinary responsibilities, transmitting news and articles with a disparaging content about RS Romania.*

*Following the measures undertaken, URMA SERGIU VIOREL has stopped writing and publishing articles abroad.*

*CHIEF OF SERVICE*    *OFFICER SPECIALIST II*
*Captain Stanescu Gabriel*   *Colonel Marinescu Dan*

Being curious to find out the real identity of Securitate sources "Cornel" and "Andrei" mentioned in this report, together with others I came across in my dossier, I signed a petition asking the council to desecretize their code names for me, as stipulated by the law. I was told that I'd have to wait since there are many such requests. Could it be that these sources are from my circle of friends or perhaps neighbors? Or family? I'd better wait.

A name jumps to my eyes: Marinescu. I came across it several times in my dossier. Ah, that's his real name and not a fictitious one. He was monitoring me during the years 1975–76, and he came to the AP office several times asking questions about what I was doing and threatening me with "unfavorable consequences" if I didn't cooperate. What a nice promotion for him! When I met him for the first time, he flashed his Securitate ID card before my eyes, saying his name was Matei and that he was a captain. Ten years later he was a colonel. He was a fair-haired man, about forty years old and with a charming smile—when he didn't hunt for "enemies" of the regime under every stone.

"What details do you want about me? I am working by myself and I send my stories to our bureau in Vienna, the editing hub for Central and Eastern Europe, sans the Soviet Union that is a separate entity. The Vienna editors are handling my reports, filing them on to the European wire, and the stories come back to Romania via Agerpres, the government-run news agency, with which AP has a contract for news and photo exchange. Everything is transparent; there's nothing to hide."

I was playing dumb with the Securitate officers, but I knew what the purpose of their visits was: they wanted me to tell them if I had contacts with American diplomats or with any foreigners and, if so, to report them to the Securitate. They were interested to learn about my sources, and they wanted to intimidate me and make sure I was aware that they were keeping me under surveillance.

My answers to their questions were uninspiring, to say the least. "Yes, I talk with American diplomats by phone strictly on press issues; my sources are Agerpres, the state-run newspapers and magazines, and various government officials."

He realized that he couldn't get much from me, and the last time he came to the office he lost his temper and told me bluntly: "I see that you don't want to help us. However, let me tell you this: without the Securitate our country could not exist. We work for Romania, for its independence." He then opened the door and went out.

Why was he telling me this nonsense? I thought he was referring to the tussle between the Soviet intelligence operatives in the country and the Romanian counterintelligence. That was the task of *Unitatea Militara* 0110, the so-called "anti-KGB unit," which was part of the 3rd Directorate. Romania was the only Warsaw Pact country that had a special department charged with spying on Soviet diplomats, many of whom were actually undercover agents working for the KGB.

After each visit by the Securitate, I used to make short notes on their questions and on my answers. Reading what was in my dossier and based on the substance of the conversations I recalled, I realize that the real person that claimed to be Matei was actually Dan Marinescu.

I check the list of names of the former officers and collaborators published by the National Council for the Study of the Securitate Archives, and I look for Marinescu. I find him. He was born in 1932 in Bucharest. From 1953 until 1988, when he retired, he worked in counterintelligence. He was a happy retiree when he was only fifty-six years old, living on a large pension—larger than what most Romanians were getting. And he lived a life of ease, probably without any financial worries, for another twenty-three years until his death in 2011. May the Maker rest his soul and may He forgive the sins Marinescu committed in his virtuous profession of uncovering and isolating the enemies of the regime.

Reading the Securitate report, I start laughing. What astonishes me is the neo-Stalinist language they used. "The stopping of the hostile activity," or "some problems facing our society, presented in a tendentious and disparaging way in the foreign press" (such as the obligation of Romanians to register their typewriters with the police), or the "biased" story about Calciu, a Romanian Orthodox priest and lifelong political dissident, in which I "wanted to present Calciu as a victim of the regime..."

The typewriter decree was designed to curb clandestine leaflets critical of Ceausescu, and heavy fines were prescribed for the illicit use of the keyboard. In order to identify the authors of these leaflets, the Securitate needed the imprints of all the typewriters existing in the country.[1]

What a scoundrel I was!

I also notice, however, a certain progress compared with the Stalinist 1950s, when for "suspicions" of having "dubious ties" with Western diplomats and "preoccupations to gather and transmit abroad data with a

---

1 Google search: Associated Press: "In Romania, typewriter called 'dangerous weapon.'"

tendentious and disparaging content for our country through the intermediary of Associated Press" one could be sentenced to twenty-five years' imprisonment—like in Kirschen's case, my Romanian predecessor.

That's where one can see the Ceausescu regime's great progress achieved in Romania. The Securitate "organs" (as the officers were formally called) were watching you closely. They tried to intimidate you, phoned you at home or at the office to complain, called you "Judas," cursed you, summoned you to the Foreign Ministry to display their proletarian disgust for your stories, but they did not torture you physically any more, and they didn't lock you up without clear proof. So, the existence of mere "suspicions" were not enough to yank you from your civilian life and land you in prison, without the presentation of some hard evidence and a public trial.

If the word "spy" is mentioned only once in my dossier, "treason" was used two or three times. A "Plan of Measures" dated November 7, 1984, which was approved by Col. Gheorghe Diaconescu, was called to "clarify the suspicions of treason in favor of the American information service." In addition, it called for the "harming of [my] character² and [my] removal" from the AP office in Bucharest. The plan also demanded "[my] persuasion to give up the writing and transmitting of unfavorable news about RS Romania."

Easier said than done.

Stretching four typewritten pages, the plan presented eleven measures to stop me from doing my job—including my "slandering vis-à-vis other foreign reporters and the management of the Associated Press agency."

Listed as "no. 3" was this piece of thinking: "For the gradual slandering of [Urma] vis-à-vis the American diplomats accredited in Bucharest and above all the ambassador and the minister-counselor, the source 'TUDORA' will be adequately instructed to feed them information of a damaging nature." Who was Tudora? A Romanian employee of the embassy or an American diplomat "bought" by the Securitate?

At number six was this measure: "For his discrediting with American reporters, sources 'PLOP' and 'CORINA' will place information to smear

---

2 Character assassination, that is.

[Urma's] competency and create serious doubts about his professional probity."

The Securitate even had a plan for my wife, who was a schoolteacher. "From among the colleagues of [Urma's] wife a source will be recruited through the intermediary of whom we will act not only to control her activity but also to spread inaccurate information [about her] to be fed to her husband."

I think, "You thickheaded, dim-witted bastards! You wanted to badmouth me vis-à-vis the AP management in New York? How do you think you could do such a thing? How could you get there? Honestly speaking, would my managers believe you or me?"

"Moreover, the thing about my wife is a scurvy trick! Is this how you use your 'disinformation information'? You mix the whole family in the same pot? Scumbags!"

Reading all this in my dossier, I start swearing. I am turning the air blue, and I cannot stop. Only, I am cursing with my mouth shut so I don't disturb the others perusing their Securitate files in the reading room at the National Council for the Study of the Securitate Archives. I am swearing. I am a Romanian; now I am not an American. There are only three or four short curse words in English, which are of little help when you want to vent your frustration or anger. In this regard, Romanian, like Russian, Hungarian, or Polish languages, gives you plenty of linguistic room to create and adapt. In this part of the world people don't shoot firearms like in America: they shoot invectives. My curses, very detailed and to the point, are exploding like bullets from a machine gun.

I recall an epigram by Pastorel Teodoreanu, a Romanian poet, humorist, gastronome, and one-time political prisoner, who spent two years in jail for his incisive and witty anti-communist lyrics.

> At Stalin's death, big tears I shed
> At a perspective all too gritty,
> As we'll be made to kiss instead
> The asses of a whole Committee.[3]

---

3   English version by Constantin Roman, London, 2010.

I start laughing, and I cannot stop. Kissing the behinds of several hundred members of the Communist Party Central Committee was no easy or pleasant undertaking. I look around the reading room where a dozen Romanians are perusing their Securitate files and all of them look absorbed and somber. I am the only one laughing. Two Council employees working in the room look at me curiously.

"The Securitate assholes," I say still laughing, pointing to my bulky dossier. What bothered them was that in my dispatches I reported the facts of daily life in Romania, the widespread food shortages, the lack of heat in people's homes in winter, the lack of elementary freedoms, Ceausescu's personality cult, and so on. That's why they considered me a "traitor" and wanted to remove me from my job—because I was describing the reality that they tried to hide or embellish.

The opening of a *DUI* file was a critical decision, being a "superior form of surveillance through the use of more complex (and) efficient means," according to the directory of words and abbreviations used by the former Securitate and now made public by the Council. Probably they wanted to charge me with treason, but they needed irrefutable proof.

It is not true that I stopped sending stories from Bucharest; I simply didn't byline them until my departure from Romania.

I look again at the first page where Col. Gheorghe Diaconescu scribbled a few words in the upper left-hand corner: "Finalize the plan with tasks to uncover and document the illicit activity of [Urma].

I check a list with Securitate officers posted on the internet, and I find Diaconescu's name. He was a former colonel in the 3rd Directorate (Counterintelligence). After Ceausescu's demise in December 1989, he became—for a short time—a deputy director of Securitate's successor, the Romanian Intelligence Service. Interesting! However, he was fired from that position for illegal possession of documents belonging to the former Securitate, for heavy drinking, and for improper handling of foreign-currency funds.

After that, Cornel Bobic, a controversial businessman, hired him to ensure the "communication protection" of his dealings. More interesting! This Bobic was one of the best-known racketeers in the 1990s. For a time he was a shareholder of Prima TV station, a confidante of Adrian Nastase, and a member of the governing Social Democratic Party (the successor of the Communist Party).

What an interesting trio: the ex-Securitate colonel Diaconescu, the shady dealer Bobic, and Nastase—aptly nicknamed *sapte case* (seven houses), a former Romanian prime minister, who later on would be imprisoned for corruption.

Only a few of the Securitate officers were really smart, the brightest being selected to work in counterintelligence in the country or in espionage abroad. They were *la crème de la crème*, those with the highest IQ. But what about the everyday political police for all citizens of the socialist republic, the blokes from "The Eye and Ear Cooperative," those from the lower ranks?

How did I contact Father Gheorghe Calciu? I phoned him. Where did I find his telephone number? Right in the Bucharest phone directory, published by the authorities. There were unconfirmed reports that he had been released after five years of prison, but officials were mum. So I picked up the phone book and found his name and number listed for everybody to see. The tired voice of an elderly and suffering man answered my call. I asked him if he was Father Calciu and he said yes. I told him who I was, and I asked him if he wanted to answer a couple of questions for an AP story. He said "yes." At the end of the call, I thanked him, and I wished him good health. I started to write a brief piece that I telexed to our Vienna bureau. The editors moved it quickly on to the European wire, and then my headaches started.

In the evening, Radio Free Europe transmitted my interview back to the country, and everybody learned about Father Calciu's release from prison and of his harsh time there. The *Voice of America* correspondent in Vienna called me to ask how I contacted Calciu. I told him that I phoned him. He tried to do the same, but the Securitate had been alerted, and Calciu's phone was disconnected. Why didn't the "blue-eyed boys" consider cutting the line as soon as Calciu arrived home from prison? Somebody must have paid a price for this "negligence." They weren't too smart, were they?

On page 174 of my Securitate dossier, I found this typewritten report, written exactly as follows:

*03.09. 1984 - 17.00*
*04.09. 1984 - 10.00*

*(In handwriting: Postul de radio "Europa Libera")*

*as part of the news bulletin at 17.00 [5 p.m.], edited by luiza cunea and read by alexandra polizu, it was transmitted:*

*bucharest—romanian priest gheorghe calciu-dumitreasa stated that his release after 5 years' imprisonment was unexpected and that the reason for that was never explained to him. father calciu made this statement in a telephone interview with =associated press= news agency. in connection with the conditions of detention, he said that in the first three years they were particularly harsh and unimaginable for someone who lives in the west. in the last two years the conditions improved. father calciu refused to give details. he told the =a.p.= correspondent that upon his release he was warned that he will be rearrested if he continued to make trouble. father calciu said that he and his wife live in permanent fear and that he never leaves home unaccompanied. in connection with his living conditions, father calciu said that they are poor because he must make ends meet on his wife's pension of 2,000 lei [$144 a month]. he asked the romanian patriarchy to reinstate him as a priest at radu voda church in bucharest, but that he didn't receive an answer to his request. father calciu [said] he was not excommunicated. at the end of the interview, he thanked all western organizations which worked for his release. father calciu also said he does not know what he will do in the future.*

This was the Securitate written account of my AP interview with Father Calciu.

I was waiting for the consequences.

"Radio Free Europe," which played a critical role in Cold War-era Eastern Europe, was 22 million Romanians' favorite broadcasting station and their only politically uncensored source of information of what was going on in their country and abroad. Ceausescu viewed it as a serious threat, and the regime waged a vindictive war against it along the years, attacking several Romanian journalists working for the US-funded radio station at its headquarters in Munich, Germany.

Therefore, I was waiting.

The next day, I received a phone call from the "blue-eyed boys" from the 3rd Directorate. Captain Sandulescu came to the AP office and asked me bluntly why I called Calciu and wrote that story. I always had an answer prepared for any circumstance, so I answered him innocently: "What's wrong with that? Father Calciu was released from prison and not sent to prison; therefore, it's a good thing to inform everybody about that, including President Reagan" who had personally pressed Ceausescu for his release.

Sandulescu—or who knows what his real name was—bristled. He grinned, showing his big, yellowish teeth. "You shouldn't have done it. You can get into trouble," he said.

"Had I not done it, somebody else could have released the story first, perhaps the *Voice of America* or *Agence France Presse*. At least AP has a permanent office in Bucharest; the others are covering Romania from Vienna or Belgrade. It's good that the story carried a Bucharest dateline," I answered.

"Calciu was too critical. You could have softened his words. You can be held responsible for spreading anti-state propaganda," the captain said, his eyes flashing with anger.

"What are you talking about? I could not change what he said, that's not how the AP works. Quotes are … quotes. One cannot doctor them," I answered.

Calciu was even more "critical" than Sandulescu thought. He told me that the main dish one summer was spinach, served with such "ingredients" as sand and worms. Other times they were given to eat such delicacies as cow's lips with the hair still on them, which were carried to the Aiud prison in central Transylvania in open trucks and stinking awfully.

Sandulescu did not make other comments. He took out a notebook and began scribbling something.

"Listen," he said, "how certain are you that you talked with Calciu? What proof do you have? Did you tape-record the interview?"

"No," I said, "but it was him. I am positive."

"What if it was not him?" he asked again.

"It was Father Calciu," I insisted.

I was thinking that it would have been better to have recorded the interview with Calciu, but I'm sure that the Securitate did record it for their purposes. I had no doubts about that. The AP office phone was tapped, same as Father Calciu's. I thought, "You know very well that I talked to him." But I didn't say anything aloud.

"Be careful what you're writing about. Don't take it as a threat," he warned me. He put his notebook in his pocket and left. After he departed, I jotted down the highlights of our conversation, just to call to my mind our meeting over the years.

I'm reading Sandulescu's three-page report in my dossier after his visit: Urma "categorically refused to give me a copy of his story of the interview sent by telex, saying it belongs to the agency and that he cannot hand over something that doesn't belong to him." That's true. I told Sandulescu to ask the state-run news agency Agerpres for a copy, which had a formal contract for news and photos exchange with AP. I was not going to give it to him.

The dull Bucharest phone directory, perhaps as dull as the city itself, was a valuable source of information in those times. That's where I found Paul Goma's address. Goma was a well-known dissident writer and leading opponent of the regime before the downfall of Ceausescu in 1989. When Larry Gerber, the AP Vienna bureau chief, came to Bucharest on one of his regular visits, we went to visit Goma straight from the airport without stopping at the hotel first. While Larry climbed the stairs to Goma's apartment, I waited downstairs in the car. Luckily, Goma was at home, and Larry talked to him. The visit was not prearranged, lest the authorities be alerted.

In Father Calciu's case, he was one of the Romanians most persecuted by the communist regime, spending a total of twenty-one years behind bars, in some of the most notorious political prisons of the time: Pitesti, Aiud, and Jilava. He was first jailed in 1948, when he was only twenty-one years old and a medical student, because he made speeches against the newly installed regime.

"We protested atheism, the collectivization of the means of production, destruction of the intelligentsia and the bourgeoisie," he told the

*Washington Post.* "The Communists did not support this, and I was put in prison for sixteen years."[4]

He was jailed again after he announced plans to give a series of seven sermons in the winter of 1978 at the Radu Voda Church in Bucharest. The sermons, which attacked Ceausescu's religious persecutions and the flattening of churches, enjoyed a large audience of young Romanians.

Prison the second time was much worse. "Ceausescu saw me as his personal enemy," Father Calciu said in his *Washington Post* interview. "For this he applied to me special methods of torture."

When he did not break, Calciu would recount later that the Securitate decided to have him killed by two cellmates—convicted murderers who had been promised leniency if they would kill him. He was made to stand in a corner of the cell and not allowed to eat, drink, speak, or relieve himself without permission, and he was often beaten. Nevertheless, he survived.

Throughout Father Calciu's imprisonment, the Reagan administration lobbied Ceausescu for his release. In August 1983, those efforts—and the dictator's fear that the United States would rescind its most-favored-nation trading status—led to the priest's release.

Calciu spent the next two years under house arrest before he was allowed to leave the country in 1985, with his wife and son. He died in the United States in 2006 at the age of eighty. His body was brought back and buried at the Petru Voda Monastery in Neamt County, in northeastern Romania.

*Requiescat in pace*, Father Calciu. You were an amazing human being and a brilliant example for your Romanian contemporaries and for future generations.

And I am so happy I had the luck and honor to be able to talk to you and to make public your "permanent fear" and your reticence to "leave home unaccompanied."

Who knows what the Securitate planned to do when you were walking out on the street, as they were very good at staging unexpected "traffic accidents."

---

4 Patricia Sullivan, "Rev. Gheorghe Calciu, 80; was called hero for protests against Ceausescu," *Washington Post*, November 27, 2006.

*The [communist] throne is not taken by the most competent dignitaries devoted to the people. Those who come to power are usually skillful schemers, masters of intrigues and corruption.*

—FYODOR BURLATSKY, RUSSIAN POLITICAL SCIENTIST

Costinesti
Summer 1968

On the Romanian Black Sea coast at Costinesti, the gray day promised little to sun worshipers. Dark clouds had covered the sky after midnight, and at daybreak a continuous and dreary drizzle started to fall.

I was awakened by my roommate who was listening to his small transistor radio. The news was about the Warsaw Pact troops' invasion of Czechoslovakia. We dressed quickly and made our way to the students' cafeteria to have our breakfast: brown bread, butter, marmalade, and a cup of tea.

On our way, we saw small groups of young Czechs who had come to spend their summer vacation on the Romanian Riviera. Their faces were gloomy, and some of them were crying.

Costinesti was Czech and Polish youths' favorite seaside resort in Romania. Several pop-music bands from Prague gave daily concerts at local restaurants, playing the latest Beatles hits and enjoying a tremendous success.

In 1968 I was a student in my senior year in the English Language Department of the University of Bucharest, and I liked to sing and play the piano. My biggest dream was to become an opera singer. However, my voice was not good enough, so I had to content myself with what I managed to find around me: the choir of the Communist Youth Union, for instance.

I recalled the cold and tense atmosphere when the young Czechs were greeted in Bulgaria at the World Festival of Youth and Students—the olympics of communist propaganda sponsored by Moscow. The festival in Sofia, where I participated as a member of the CYU choir, had ended three weeks before the Soviet tanks conquered Prague.

Before we left Romania, Ion Iliescu—one of the young officials in Ceausescu's entourage and a Cabinet minister—told us that Bucharest followed the liberalization reforms in Czechoslovakia under Dubcek's Prague Spring "with interest and sympathy."

Iliescu was one of the dignitaries who appeared less impressed with the personality cult that Ceausescu, the former shoemaker apprentice and teenage drifter, was stubbornly building for himself.

Nevertheless, Iliescu was an ambitious apparatchik and a pureblood Marxist-Leninist bell cow, never a regime dissident who would strive to rid Romania of communism.

Simply said, Iliescu envied Ceausescu for his top job, and he would swallow his Communist Party card to take his place. That would happen twenty years later under different circumstances. In 1968, however, Iliescu was not yet the "skillful schemer" disguised as a democrat who would be willing to steer the country from communism to capitalism.

Honesty and honor are rarely rewarded in politics. If political winds change direction, from East to West and from West to East, why bother? Machiavelli, the father of *realpolitik*, was a sucker compared to the great intriguers and conspirators of communism.

For me, at least, it's a mystery why Ceausescu did not totally remove Iliescu from political life as he did with some of his other opponents, only demoting him to lesser positions. How come the "Genius of the Carpathians" didn't see in Iliescu the danger that he would have to face, when everybody—including the Securitate—knew for years that Iliescu would replace him? Was Ceausescu afraid of Moscow's reaction? Perhaps this is the only explanation.

Iliescu's father, a communist member when the Party was banned in the country for its pro-Moscow policies, had fled to the Soviet Union in 1930 where he spent five years in hiding.

A Soviet Union admirer in his turn, Iliescu would spend several years in Moscow to study hydraulics, a topic in applied science and engineering dealing with the mechanical properties of liquids. For a future politician, hydraulics is a great choice. Iliescu would be more fluid than water and more slippery than a fish. What's more fluid than politics? He would know how to avoid getting under Ceausescu's skin and live quietly in his aquarium, waiting patiently for his time to come. Who would have thought that from a fish he would turn into a shark?

The day before we departed to Sofia, in a theater hall of a students' campus in Bucharest, Iliescu urged us to be friendly with our Czech colleagues, even if the Bulgarian hosts gave them the cold shoulder.

"Our country regards with sympathy the efforts of the Czechoslovak people to advance on the road of socialist construction," Iliescu told us, singing the musical score written by Ceausescu.

Iliescu's words proved prophetic. In Sofia, only the Romanians will be cordial to the young Czechs and Slovaks.

The problem was not how friendly we were supposed to be with the Czechs. Two years before, in an effort to ensure "normal demographic growth" after complaining that there were not enough Romanians, Ceausescu had signed Decree 770 that banned abortions for women younger than forty-five or who delivered less than four children, placing Romanians' sexuality under the control of the Communist Party.[5] With contraceptives disappearing from pharmacy shelves, it was tough to find a

---

5 Ceausescu's Decree 770 proved to be a shameful disaster for Romania. Due to worsening economic conditions, the government would be unable to provide assistance in the form of childcare centers and accessible medical care. Unwanted children were born, and, as their parents could not afford to care for them, they were abandoned in hospitals or orphanages. Securitate agents were placed in gynecological wards, while regular pregnancy tests were made mandatory for women of childbearing age to make sure they didn't hide their pregnancies or use contraceptives. At least 9,400 women would die due to complications arising from illegal abortions, according to official figures. In December 1989, when Ceausescu was toppled, about 100,000 children lived in orphanages in inhumane conditions.

sexual partner. Romanians laughed at their misfortune and made political jokes, knowing they could not change anything:

When Gheorghiu Dej was Party head
We were banging on every bed
And our dongs were infrared.
Now comrade Ceauses-**koo**
Says we're in deep **doo-doo**!

Did Iliescu, the Cabinet minister in charge of "youth problems," do anything to ease the restrictions of the anti-abortion diktat? No. Sex was considered a silly game, not a serious problem like the patriotic duty of procreating more Romanians. People would figure out a way to find enjoyment! In our case, we sang patriotic songs in the Communist Youth Union choir. It provided escapism in a way, though it didn't suck our energy.

I recalled the bus trip from Bucharest to Sofia, the dusty Bulgarian roads, the poor villages, and the many slogans hanging from houses' walls or at street intersections. Most of them praised the heroic Soviet people and the unshakeable Bulgarian-Soviet friendship.

"Eternal brotherhood with the Soviet Union," said one in red block letters on a banner that hung across a local road, from lamppost to lamppost. "The Soviet Union is the world guarantor of peace," said another. Hundreds of other slogans along the roads were of the same standard variety. "Glory to the Bulgarian Communist Party," said another, offering an indication where the population still needed ideological reinforcement.

We were proud that slogans praising the Soviet Union were no longer displayed in Romania, after Bucharest began a slow disengagement from Moscow domination in the early 1960s and the study of the Russian language in schools ceased to be mandatory.

Sofia, nestled at the base of the Vitosha Mountains and dominated by the Alexander Nevsky Orthodox Cathedral, was festively bedecked and spruced up for the festival—a political carnival organized by Moscow where "progressive" youths from all over the world would take part. Apart from eating, drinking, and dancing, these brave fighters for peace were vehemently denouncing US imperialism and the military aggression in Vietnam.

*Fielding's Travel Guide to Europe* summed up Bulgaria's tourist attractions in several lines. Actually, they were not even mentioned. The problem was how to get an entrance visa.

"The Homeland Front," said the tourist guide, "will be pleased to give you a visa if you can prove that (1) you are morally honest, (2) politically correct, and (3) your brother-in-law is Nikita S. Khrushchev. Otherwise, you have a one-in-ten-billion chance."

Well, getting an entry visa to Bulgaria wasn't a problem for us, despite the fact that Khrushchev had been removed from power four years before.

For us the trip to Sofia left pleasant memories. The memories were fortified by our view of the Bulgarian teenage hostesses, friendly, talkative, and endowed with generous boobs, who greeted us in hostels and restaurants. We learned on this occasion that the festival had produced severe food shortages across Bulgaria because the best food staples had to be put aside for the hungry and high-spirited visitors.

The Czechs usually walked in clusters, preferring the group ambiance to individual tourism. They felt isolated. The Bulgarian hosts didn't miss any occasion to show them that their presence at the festival was tolerated but not welcomed. A jazz band from Prague was not allowed to give a concert that had been planned, and they were only permitted to perform after the Czech delegation lodged a formal protest and threatened with withdrawal from the anti-imperialist pageant.

The day after the Kremlin-led invasion, in which Romania refused to take part, scores of Czech tourists in Bulgaria were expelled to neighboring Romania.

"Go to your Romanian friends," Bulgarian custom officials told them scornfully, before kicking them out of the country. Some of them, who protested the treatment, were roughed up. I saw them coming to Costinesti from the nearby border in their old Skodas, and tears were streaming down their tanned faces.

After Ceausescu's anti-Soviet speech in Bucharest, Romanians hosted the Czechs in their homes and gave them food and money until their return home.

I listened to Ceausescu's speech on my friend's small radio, and I was proud I was a Romanian. After several days, I took the train back to Bucharest, although my vacation voucher issued by the Communist Students' Association allowed me to spend another week in Costinesti. Singing officially acclaimed hymns in the choir of the Communist Youth Union was a highly respected pursuit and had its advantages.

The train was overcrowded, and I found standing room near a car door in the second class. Some were saying that several tanks from Bucharest's military garrison had been seen on some streets, but their destination was a mystery.

The sun was descending toward sunset over the vast Dobrogea Plain, on which clusters of trees stabbed the wilderness here and there. It resembled a huge, red globe hanging miraculously in the air.

Leaning against the door window, I was thinking of my life, which was flowing slowly and drearily like a river crossing a plain. I had the taste of my own mediocrity in my mouth, and the feeling of failure was overwhelming.

After high school, my parents wanted me to study piano at the Conservatory. In our family classical music was highly esteemed. My mother was trained as a pianist in Paris for a while, but after she got married, family chores and her children's education left her little time to hone her artistic career.

I couldn't practice more than two hours a day. That didn't dampen my parents' hopes to see me a pianist. I didn't have patience for study, and I lacked the motivation to succeed in my life. The scales and arpeggios bored me to death. I was devoid of artistic ambitions, and the future was not among my concerns.

Eventually I decided to study English language and literature at the University. I had one more year until graduation...and then the unknown. What job would I find? Some of my colleagues were making translations for literary publications, hoping to be hired after graduation. Others had the attention of the Securitate, which was interested in hiring them as English teachers or translators for their employees, though not as civilians.

Nothing interested me except opera music and my thoughts, and nobody bothered me. I didn't have any concerns and ambitions, and I was waiting for my future with indifference and a feeling of foolish confidence without any real support.

"To hell with the future. It's better to talk about the present," said somebody whose name I cannot remember. "The future can be a very dangerous excuse. It gives you the pretext to do awful things in the present." Six million Jews were exterminated in the name of the future. *Macho* Marx developed his economic and social theory thinking about the golden future of the proletariat.

The future is dangerous. Let's talk only about the present. How is the present? Boring.

For me the job I would find after graduation was a foggy and remote thing. Practically, it had no importance. Why should I be concerned about my future?

It was almost dark when we arrived in Bucharest's *Gara de Nord.* I took my small suitcase and made for the exit. There were no distinct signs of tension. Outside the station, cars were blaring their horns and shrieking their brakes. Across from the station, the Gypsy flower sellers were doing their usual noisy business.

"What's going on here?" I asked a man who was reading the evening paper. "How big of a threat are the Russians?"

The man folded the paper and, after he put it in one of the pockets of his tattered jacket, answered quietly: "The Russians? The Americans will turn them into minced meat."

Pacified somewhat, I hopped in a bus and headed for home.

My family was sitting around the radio listening to Free Europe to keep abreast of the latest developments from Prague. Dubcek had been put on a plane and transported to Moscow where Brezhnev was waiting to roast him for his Prague Spring liberal reforms. The question was how would he return from Moscow: alive or in a coffin?

A heavy, depressing atmosphere hung over the city. Would the Warsaw Pact armies invade Romania like Czechoslovakia, or not?

As far as I was concerned, I had one more month of vacation until my rendezvous with Shakespeare and company.

## 3

*It's a world of laughter*
*A world of tears.*
*It's a world of hopes*
*And a world of fears.*

—Children's song "It's a Small World"
Lyrics by Slim Whitman

Bucharest and Sapanta
Summer 1968

In the next few days, Bucharest was stormed not by the Warsaw Pact armies but by the hordes of Western reporters, drawn by Romania's independent stance and by Ceausescu's daring speech.

The legendary English Bar at Athénée Palace cordially greeted everyone with its vast collection of whisky, gin, Italian vermouth, French cognac, and other imported drinks. This was the venue where news, rumors, and jokes were exchanged like in the old days.

Calea Victoriei, Romania's version of Broadway, had survived the war without major losses. Only the National Theatre, a gem of the acoustics of the nineteenth century, was destroyed by *Luftwaffe* in a punishing air raid as payback for Romania's switching sides and joining the Allied forces in August 1944. Fortunately, the Telephones Palace escaped unscathed. A true skyscraper for prewar Bucharest, the building was the work of two American architects in the early 1930s, and for a time it was the tallest construction in the country. The sprawling marble hall, the huge and elegant staircase, and the large windows gave the Palace a capitalist aura transplanted to the garrulous and gossip-loving Bucharest.

Dominated by *Palatul Telefoanelor*, the meandering Calea Victoriei still maintained some of the elegant appearance of the good life before the war due to several pricey restaurants, theaters, and fashion boutiques. In the former days of glory, when the *Galeries Lafayette* department store was built, these stores displayed *le dernier écrit de la mode*, which in Romanians' case—as enthusiastic worshipers at the shrine of the French culture—always used to come from Paris.

Not far from the telephones building was the Palace Square, dominated by the former royal residence, the National Library, built in the neo-classical French style, and the Communist Party headquarters, which before the Second World War housed the Ministry of the Interior equipped with a sprawling police interrogation center with hundreds of cells on three levels underground. This was the first institution taken over by the Soviet Red Army and Romanian communist forces after the war.

At the northern end of the old artery was Piata Victoriei. Flanked by the imposing building of the Foreign Ministry, the large, cobblestoned square would get some international acclaim after world leaders such as President Gerald Ford, Hua Guofeng of China, and Mikhail Gorbachev will become Ceausescu's political dancing partners of the *hora* dance in the years to come.

At Athénée Palace Hotel, one of the most notorious and stylish nests of international spies and informers in Europe before World War II, Roy Higgins, Tom Browne, and Patrick Wood (not their real names)—correspondents of US and British newspapers and press agencies—had just sent out their written dispatches about Ceausescu's anti-Kremlin speech. Nursing several bottles of beer in the English Bar, they were reviewing the day's events.

Browne, tall and elegant, dominated the room with his large head covered in red hair; he looked like a character taken from Walter Scott's novels about medieval England. He was the East European correspondent of a New York newspaper, and Romanian officials viewed his presence in Bucharest with respect. They were happy that their country was drawing so much American interest for its daring stand in the Czech-Soviet conflict. The hosts were jumping up with satisfaction at seeing so many

Western reporters and rightfully so. Ceausescu was flattered and proud whenever his activities called the attention of the free world.

"The latest rumor is that bloody clashes took place between Romanian and Soviet border guards," said Browne, taking a big gulp from a bottle. He went on: "I was told that several Romanian army men were shot because they had been under orders not to answer the provocations. I can hardly believe such a thing really happened."

Rumors like this were the Romanians' daily bread. The old Levantine custom to eavesdrop on other people's conversations, distrust everybody while trusting only their own opinions and suspecting a conspiracy behind every tree is a characteristic of those living in this part of the world. These people are eager to know what's going on around them, but they don't care if the information they get is entirely accurate. A piece of information is a piece of information, accurate or not. Where do the facts end? Where does the fiction start? Romanians' thirst for detail and a natural inclination to hyperbole, blather, and gossip rendered the sorting operation difficult.

According to some reports, the army had recently obtained a secret weapon in its arsenal, a "killer light beam" capable of melting the thick armor plate of tanks. With the help of the "blinding beam," several Soviet tanks that had crossed the border in northern Romania were turned into a heap of smoldering rubble. There were no details about the frightening Romanian "stream of light," but the rumor had it that it was laser powered. Henri Coanda,[6] a pioneer of world aviation and a prominent physicist, was said to have conceived the weapon.

Coanda spent almost his entire life in England and France. A brilliant mind, he became technical manager of Bristol Aeroplane Company when he was only twenty-six years old. He became sentimental in his old age and was attracted to his native country, and Ceausescu invited him to spend his last years in Bucharest. Coanda was given a lavish mansion in

---

6 After the 1989 revolution, the Romanian-born scientist would lend his name to Bucharest's main international airport, known before as Otopeni. See an explanation in Chapter 12.

the heart of the city and a building near *Piata Romana* where he started a research institute. To reward such a warm reception, the old and energetic scientist—credited by some as building the world's first jet—felt obliged to contribute something to Romania. Thus, he supposedly offered his conationals his last great invention: a killer laser beam.

"This rumor seems to be promoted by the government to bolster the morale of the people and boost their confidence in the leadership," said Wood, a British press agency man. "The question is will the Russians buy this? Certainly not. They know perfectly well what's in the weapons storehouse of their allies. It smells of cheap fiction."

Thin, tall, and walking with a limp, Wood, whose father had been the Balkan correspondent of a London paper before the war, continued: "The most ridiculous thing is that Romanian officials neither confirm nor deny these rumors. They only smile and raise their shoulders. How can you trust them?

"Romania is the country in Europe that nobody takes seriously," added Wood. "Hemingway, the reporter, said this in a magazine article."

"Probably Hemingway based his assertion on the dancing game of Romania in the two world wars when they waltzed with both camps by turns," said Higgins. Higgins, who sported a nicely trimmed black beard, was writing for a US news wire.

"At the start of the last war, the Romanians allied themselves with Nazi Germany to get back Bessarabia from the Soviets, and then realizing that Hitler would lose the battle, they quickly switched sides and joined the Allies. Loyalties change here as quickly as the weather in the mountains," concluded Higgins.

"As a matter of fact, the groundwork of Romanian politics has been to keep a foot in both camps," added Browne, prying open another bottle of beer. "Today with *these* guys, tomorrow with *the other* guys, and so on. Romanians have in their DNA the cult of compromise, or should I say duplicity. There's no culture of honor here, like in Poland."

After a brief pause, he went on: "It's a small but rich country that has been cherished by many empires along the centuries. The illiterate peasants, the majority of the population at any time, have always been robbed. The politicians and businessmen were corrupt, thinking only of their personal gain—how to get rich, by any means. Bribery and disloyalty worked better than in other parts of Eastern Europe. Perhaps this was the upshot of four centuries of Turkish domination, but the sultans in Istanbul found a fertile ground here to promote their interests."

Wood smiled and said ironically: "Well, the communists settled the corruption problem after the war, once and for all, didn't they? They either imprisoned the former wealthy class, the so-called bourgeoisie, or confiscated their properties. As simple as that."

Little by little, the bar's clientele thinned out. At two corner tables, several "night birds"—the Romanian word for hookers—working the late shift, were talking and smoking, still waiting for their usual customers.

At seven o'clock most people were hurrying to get back home earlier than usual to listen to Radio Free Europe. In the diffuse light of the sunset, the old hotel, a stone's throw from the former Royal Palace, seemed to enjoy a second life. One of the most celebrated European hotels and the swankiest in the Balkans, Athénée Palace inspired many Western writers.

The *Newsweek* correspondent, R. G. Waldek, wrote a book in 1942 with the setting of the hotel in a Bucharest that had become the focal point of European intelligence services. Bucharest was depicted as a depraved and unfortunate capital where the desire to look Western combined with the charm and nostalgia of the fuzzy lights of the Levant. The hotel also figured prominently in Olivia Manning's bestseller *The Balkan Trilogy*, which described a Bucharest throbbing with the tensions of war until the war itself engulfed Romania. In the somber setting of disintegration, the British writer created tragicomedy of the highest order. Pre-war Bucharest was the capital of rumors, betrayals, political intrigues, arrests, a stage on which human absurdity was magnified by the deadly seriousness of its context.

In 1948 the hotel was nationalized by the new communist regime and in the early '50s, with the help of the Soviet KGB, it was outfitted with the most advanced eavesdropping and monitoring technologies and turned into a Romanian "espionage factory."

Here is how Dan Halpern portrays the Marxist-Leninist conversion of the hotel in "The Walls Have Ears," an article published in *Travel & Leisure* magazine:

> " ... Bugs were installed in every room. The phones were tapped. In the café and the restaurant and the bar, even the ashtrays were said to be equipped with microphones. The busboys were watching; the waiters were listening. In the lobby, the bellboys and the concierge and the receptionists were all on the government payroll. Outside, the cabstand was run by the Securitate, Romania's secret police under communism; every pay phone within a half-mile of the hotel was tapped.
>
> That is to say, it was a thorough job. The hotel's general director was an undercover colonel in the Securitate's Counterespionage Directorate; the hotel's deputy director was a colonel in the DIE, the Romanian CIA. The doormen did surveillance; the housekeeping staff photographed all documents in the guests' rooms. The prostitutes in the lobby and in the bar and in the nightclub reported directly to their employers; the free-speaking bons vivants and Romanian intellectuals hanging around the café, not to mention a number of the guests, had been planted..." [7]

All of a sudden, the doors of the bar swung open, and several officials from the Foreign Ministry and Agerpres dashed inside. Spotting the three reporters, they rushed to them.

"Very important and urgent," said one of them, who was short and balding. His name was Timofte, and he was a secretary in the Press and Culture Department of the ministry.

"In three hours we depart by train to northern Transylvania. We'll get there by tomorrow morning," he added.

"What's the exact destination?" asked Wood. "And why the rush? What's so important?"

---

[7] Dan Halpern, "The Walls Have Ears," *Travel & Leisure* 35, no. 6 (June 2005):168, www.gobtf.com/BtF/Lodgings/Info/AthArtcl.html.

"We are going to the Soviet border," Timofte answered in a whisper, looking around to make sure there were no Moscow agents in the room.

"Where exactly?" insisted Wood.

"Sighet," the Romanian diplomat answered curtly. "To get acquainted with the splendors of our homeland. The Tourism Ministry sponsors the trip. It won't cost you a dime—except for the bottles of beer at the dining car, of course," he said, attempting to make a quick count of the number of bottles emptied by the three reporters at the bar.

Browne looked at Wood and Higgins.

"I don't understand. Why should we leave Bucharest now? What's so interesting in northern Transylvania?" he asked Timofte.

Timofte, raised and steeled at the postwar school of Romanian diplomacy, felt obliged to divulge only the pretext of the unusual invitation.

"We're going to visit a cemetery. A more special cemetery," he said with a chuckle.

The three reporters looked puzzled, not knowing how to take Timofte's words. Was it a joke? A trick to make them leave Bucharest at such a delicate time? Talleyrand, who said that diplomats have a tongue only to hide their thoughts, would have found a competent trickster in his Romanian colleague.

"Is it perhaps a cemetery of Romanian soldiers who died recently defending their country? Is it true that clashes took place with the Soviet border guards?" asked Higgins with the amateur angler's philosophy: if the fish jumps to bait, fine; if not, what do you lose?

"No, it's a cemetery of civilians…of farmers, cheerful boys and girls who died peacefully," said Timofte, bursting into laughter. "But it's still quite interesting."

Thinking that Timofte's invitation had to have a deeper meaning than a mere tourist trip, Browne and Wood decided to honor the invitation to go on the government junket. Higgins said he wanted to stay in Bucharest, just in case.

At *Gara de Nord*, the two reporters realized that their Romanian hosts had planned the excursion in a big hurry. They bought tickets at the sleeping car, the only ones available, and hopped in the night train—six Western reporters in all, who were outnumbered by the suite of Romanian diplomats and other obscure officials, who didn't bother to introduce themselves. Among the foreign journalists, there were no Soviet newsmen. The East European media, with the exception of the Yugoslav and Albanian press, had ignored Ceausescu's speech.

The train started rolling after a short while, and the reporters were given a small map of Romania and tourist folders on which was written, in big blue letters, *Welcome to the Black Sea Coast*. At daybreak they saw that the train was snaking through an alpine gorge dominated by coniferous woods on each side. The track ran parallel to a river that, according to one of the guides accompanying them, was called Viseu. Soon the gorge opened on to a plain, and the train passed a few yards from another river. They were told this one was called Tisa. On the other side of Tisa was the Soviet border, dotted with wooden watchtowers that were a stone's throw from the tracks. Their attention was also drawn to a former church whose spires and steeples had been cut off and covered by a flat tin roof. They were told that the church had been decapitated on orders from Stalin, and the building had been turned into a town hall, or "people's council" in the Leninist jargon of the time.

The scenery did not change any more since the track ran parallel with the Tisa and the Soviet border. The train was heading for Sighet, cutting through the Maramures Depression, a natural stronghold enclosed by mountains on three sides. Forests of birch, oak, and fir trees covered large areas in this part of the country, where a "wood civilization" has survived for hundreds of years.

The Maramures region, fortunately untouched by the forced industrialization that was polluting much of the rest of Romania, is a vast natural fortress where everything—from doors to houses and churches—is made of wood.

The quality of the Maramures wood was admired in Europe ever since the eighteenth century when the spruce fir began to be used for the manufacturing of violins and cellos in Vienna, the guide told them.

Passing through apple orchards, the train was nearing Sighet, the closest Romanian town to the Soviet border. Before the Second World War, Sighet was known for its large Jewish community. Elie Wiesel, a Holocaust survivor and award-wining novelist, was born in this town. In 1944, when he was fifteen years old, he and his entire family were sent to Auschwitz and other Nazi concentration camps, together with over 120,000 Jews in northwestern Transylvania, which was at that time under the jurisdiction of the Miklos Horthy regime in Hungary.[8] He lived in the camps under inhumane conditions, gradually starving, and was freed from Buchenwald in 1945. Of his relatives, only he and two of his sisters survived. In his novel *The Gates of the Forest*, published in French, he described his tragic experiences as a teenager in Sighet, where his father owned a grocery store.

After the war and the communist takeover, Sighet got an infamous reputation due to the local penitentiary. It was there where opponents of the regime were incarcerated—including three former Romanian prime ministers and scores of other politicians, academics, military officers, church leaders, journalists, and historians (many of whom were over sixty years old). It was a place of extermination for the country's elites and a maximum-security prison, with the Soviet border only a mile away. The prisoners lived in unheated cells and were not allowed to look out of the windows. Many of them died in custody.

The train slowed down and suddenly came to a halt. The morning was unusually cold. In the north, fall comes much earlier than in Bucharest. A persistent stench of stale urine greeted the visitors. The group of foreign reporters and Romanian officials crossed the old and decrepit rail station and reached a small square with dilapidated houses. Some walls had visible cracks in them and plaster damage.

On the narrow and muddy streets near the station, there were horse-drawn carts, peasant women balancing bundles on their heads, mules carrying farm gear, and a few beat-up cars, belching a black and choking smoke.

A small bus belonging to the local tourism office was parked nearby. After they boarded, they were told that their destination was Sapanta, a village near Sighet.

"But before we get there, we'd like to show you something else," said Timofte, smiling enigmatically.

---

8 Northern Transylvania, situated within the territory of Romania, was part of Hungary between 1940–1944.

The narrow road, paved but filled with potholes, was passing through small villages with the houses painted in striking colors: red, green, blue, and yellow. Wooden fences and carved tall gates in the shape of rustic arches of triumph and adorned with stylized motifs of sunflowers and birds enclosed the farmhouses, which looked deserted. There were no souls around.

Timofte told them that several Soviet tanks rolled on the other side of the border two days before the military invasion of Czechoslovakia. Their midnight rumbling could be heard from Sighet.

After a few miles, the bus stopped outside a village at an intersection of the Tisa and Iza rivers, and the reporters were told to get off. On a nearby hill, Romanian soldiers with their AK-47 rifles hanging over their shoulders were listening to an army captain with three-day-old beard stubble. The captain was explaining something to them, and his words were accompanied by short, quick hand gestures.

Several armored personnel carriers painted in dark green, with the machine guns in shooting position, and several jeeps manufactured in the country were stirring the dust on a dirt road that circled the small hill. The captain came to the foreign journalists and, after a short conversation with Timofte, told them that until several hours ago Soviet troops had been posted on the northern side of the hill. The Russians had crossed the border two days before and advanced less than a mile on the Romanian territory, until they found themselves facing the troops of the Romanian military garrison in Sighet.

The two sides looked at each other a day and a night until the Russians decided to pull back behind the border, the same night the reporters had traveled by train from Bucharest.

"Too late," said Timofte, as if attempting to find an excuse. "It would have been an interesting subject for the foreign press. But for us it's better it ended this way," he added with a sigh of relief.

The Russian troops did not come with tanks in their short incursion, coming instead on several armored personnel carriers, with an assortment of weapons.

The captain said their action was probably aimed at intimidating the Romanians, but the military units in the area did not budge. If the Russians had forced their passage to the south, across the paved road, the Romanians were under orders to resist, and bloody clashes would have taken place. Instead, only several volleys of automatic weapons were fired into the air, and nobody got hurt, the captain said.

"Had they come with their tanks, willing to start a fight, how would you have stopped them?" asked Browne. "Would you have used the mysterious laser beam that melts everything?"

The captain understood the ironic allusion but didn't blink.

"I heard that our boys turned two Soviet tanks to dust at Darabani when they crossed the border," he said. He chuckled and continued: "Here things were less complicated. After forty-eight hours the Russians pulled back peacefully."

"Bad luck," said Wood. "A photo with Romanian and Russian soldiers face-to-face, studying each other like fighting roosters would have been awesome—let alone a few bloody clashes." He pulled his Nikon camera, slung over his shoulder on a strap, and took shots of the hill where Romanian soldiers—dressed in their khaki uniforms and armed to the teeth—were mingling with a flock of sheep looking for grazing land, totally ignoring the political events of the last few days.

"Didn't I tell you that this trip serves a tourist purpose?" Timofte intervened, changing the subject "Why are the Western reporters so fascinated with war and blood? Sensational stuff sells better; isn't that it? Peace is boring, I know," he said, making a grimace.

There was a moment of silence.

"Then, if you want, let's go see the crosses we promised you last night," Timofte said seriously. "*Cherchez les morts*."

They got on the bus and headed toward Sapanta, leaving the paved road. Making a left turn, the bus entered a country road flanked on both sides by houses that hid themselves behind tall wooden fences. In Transylvania, people value their privacy more than anything else.

At the end of the road, the bus came to a stop. "You can leave your sadness at the gate," Timofte told the group of reporters before getting off. "Welcome to *Cimitirul Vesel* or the Merry Cemetery," he bellowed.

Nestled among forested hills, the grounds are dominated by several hundred gaily painted oaken crosses, many with tongue-in-cheek couplets about the life and death of the deceased.

Most of the crosses and inscriptions are the work of Stan Ioan Patras, a local master carver, who started working on them before the war. Written in the first person, each epitaph tells something about the person it represents.

After they visited the small brick-built church in the middle of the cemetery, the suite of Western reporters and Romanian officials started walking slowly among the graves, accompanied by the guides from Bucharest. The air was full of the sissing of grasshoppers. Soon the visitors became acquainted with the fate of Dumitru Holdis, a villager who died a "forced death" after consuming considerable amounts of *tsuica*, a potent brew made from plums and the biggest source of drinking excess in Romania. Wrestling with the rhyming epitaphs, Timofte began to translate into English:

Tsuica is a genuine pest,
It brings us torture and unrest
Since it brought it to me. You see,
I kicked the bucket at 43.

Fate was more lenient with another *tsuica* consumer and allowed him more time to live on earth:

Patac Gheorghe has been my name,
Both at work and merry game.
While the world was dear to us
We played prank over the glass.
While we were in our good health

We strove much to amass wealth.
Gone is now our wealth and past.
To the grave we've come at last.
I gave up my life to heaven
At the age of 77.

Beads of perspiration covered Timofte's forehead, which he wiped off with his handkerchief. Struggling with the translation of epitaphs into Shakespeare's language was a bigger torture than the consumption of *tsuica*.

One of the guides told them that the idea of mirth in death was rooted in the tradition of the Dacians, the ancestors of today's Romanians. They used to meet death laughing because they believed that another life started after their passing away. Ancient traditions and beliefs were better preserved in this isolated region girdled by mountains than elsewhere, the guide told them.

Not all of the epitaphs were funny. Prodded by the journalists, Timofte began to tell the story of a mother who forgave her son for killing her:

I have lain here since I came
Braic Ileana is my name.
Sons I had in my life five
Would God keep them all alive.
Griga, may you pardoned be
Even though you did stab me
When you came home full of beer
Well have you laid me down here
In the chapel's shade; but you
Shall some day come hither too.

Doing his best to put it into English verse, Timofte's russet-red face turned to a grimace. Sweat began to bleed through his shirt. He sighed and exhaled noisily. "Please, no more. I've had enough for today."

The reporters started laughing, though they didn't look too amused. "Nice story," Browne intervened. "You brought us here after we crossed the entire country to show us these bizarre crosses. But the real purpose wasn't tourism, was it?"

"What do you mean?" asked Timofte, anticipating the answer.

"The threat of bloody clashes with the Russians appeared imminent, and probably the most difficult moments are not over yet. Somebody had to write a story for the world to find out—but not the Romanian government-controlled press. Am I right?" said Browne.

Timofte didn't bother to answer. What could he say?

"A virtuoso performance in intrigue, deceit, and maneuvering. Masterstrokes of political management. Walking the tightrope. Daring violation of bloc discipline," said Wood with a guffaw of derisive laughter.

"And, of course, traditional mastery of tactics," added Browne, disdainfully. "The Merry Cemetery, as you call it, could be proof of your ancestors' philosophy, but if the Russians invade your country as they did in Czechoslovakia, I doubt that Romanians will meet their death lightheartedly," he said. "And I doubt they'll have the time and desire to carve painted crosses with or without epitaphs."

During those tense moments for their country, the Romanian authorities had tried to use the Western reporters to send a dramatic message to the world about Moscow's undeclared intentions.

The visit to the cemetery had been a bluff, a mere pretext to bring the reporters to the border to pull the alarm by writing about a potential conflict between Romanian and Soviet troops.

An elderly farmer dressed in local peasant garb, wearing a sheepskin and tight linen slacks, welcomed them as they left through the gate of the cemetery. He was carrying a wooden tray with a large flask of *tsuica* and a big, round loaf of bread on it.

"Welcome to Sapanta," he said. "Please break a piece of bread and take a gulp of *tsuica*. That's how we greet our guests according to our tradition."

After they passed the test of local tradition, the group got on the bus for the return trip to Sighet. The atmosphere was more relaxed, and Timofte and the other Romanian officials were in a better disposition for the first time since their departure from Bucharest.

"Remember what I'm going to tell you now," said Timofte, in his resounding voice. "In this part of the world, dramas have a cheerful undertone. Tragedies come and go, but we stay. We know that we cannot change things, and we make good cheer with drink and feasting. History was not too good to us—and neither us with history, honestly speaking. And geography placed us at the crossroads of all evils: the Russian and the Ottoman empires fighting for hegemony over our land. But we are not the worst people on earth."

There was a long pause, and then the Romanian diplomat continued: "If you want, we can make other trips like this."

A prolonged noooo! burst out of the reporters' mouths.

"Not now," said Browne. "Perhaps some other time."

"We could visit, for instance, the Danube Delta so you can see how Moscow is robbing Mother Europe of its newest land," Timofte said, shrieking with laughter.

*Tsuica* had brought him to a loquacious euphoria. For Timofte the fiery national spirit was not a "genuine pest." On the contrary, perhaps it was a source of inspiration.

"How's that?" asked a French journalist from the group.

"Let me tell you a secret. But I'm talking off the record. Don't quote me by name."

"Agreed," said Browne.

Timofte told them how every year the formerly beautiful blue Danube, now brownish in color and polluted, collects tens of thousands of tons of soil and alluvium along its way from the Black Forest in Germany toward its sprawling delta in Romania. There, it branches into three main distributaries, the biggest one bordering the Soviet Union, before flowing into the Black Sea.

"About two square kilometers of new Soviet land is added every year from the alluvium that the old river collects from Germany, Austria, Czechoslovakia, Hungary, Yugoslavia, Bulgaria, and Romania. But Moscow gets most of the new territory as well as the feces collected from the old continent. Everybody knows that the beautiful Danube is nicknamed 'Europe's latrine,'" he said, tears of laughter streaming down his red cheeks.

"And where is the rest of the shit going?" the Frenchman asked, visibly interested.

"To our country," answered Timofte. "But we are more modest. We take only a third of the loot. The lion's share is Kremlin's property. We don't complain."

The Romanian diplomat took out a flask from his briefcase and raised it like a trophy. "This is stronger than *tsuica* or *slivovitz*. They are calling it Transylvanian *palinca*, and it can blow the back of your head off. It's 60 per cent alcohol—heavy ammunition for tough situations. It cleanses your system. Who wants to try?" he asked looking around.

"I want to try it," the Frenchman said. He took a big gulp, and his throat burned in pain. "*Merde*," he exclaimed. "It's poison. Insane."

Timofte put the flask back in his briefcase, after helping himself to a mouthful.

"Everything is crazy in this part of the world. We produce more history than we can carry on our backs. Look at the Serbs," he said. "The Turks beat them at the Battle of Kosovo six hundred years ago and forced them to pay tribute to the sultan, and you know what happened? The Serbs were so proud of their defeat that they considered it a big victory and a symbol of Serbian nationalism by defending the interests and security of Christian Europe.

"Or Bulgarians and Albanians," continued Timofte unleashed. "When they nod their head, that's a sign of disapproval, while for Romanians it means OK. And when they shake it, which for us means 'no,' for them it's 'yes.' Isn't that pure madness?"

The next morning, the joyful group arrived at *Gara de Nord*, relaxed after their fact-finding trip and with a deeper understanding of the Romanians' way of thinking.

"We are at your disposal for any problem," said a sober Timofte, and he shook hands with all of them before departing. "Call me if you have a question."

# 4

*Traiasca fraternitatea Romano-Americana!*

—President Nixon, in Romanian, to Ceausescu

Bucharest
Summer 1969

A year after the rape of Czechoslovakia, I graduated from the English Language and Literature Department of Bucharest University, ending my permanent struggle with unhappy and boring scribblers like Dryden and Pope.

My diploma paper, capping five years of study, dealt with a stimulating subject: "Italian Influences in The Canterbury Tales," a collection of stories by people from all over England who prepared for a pilgrimage to the Canterbury Cathedral to receive the blessings of an English martyr.

Geoffrey Chaucer was arguably the most "Italian" English writer, as he was inspired by such writers from Italy's *Trecento* and *Quattrocento* periods as Petrarch and Boccaccio (*The Decameron*) with their taste for piquant, licentious tales.

"The Wife of Bath's Tale," who was very much in the business of marriage and had five husbands. Or "The Reeve's Tale," where two young Cambridge students took revenge on a miller who had cheated them on flour by screwing his wife and daughter and beating him to a pulp.

Leaving the Wife of Bath and the Reeve alone, Richard Milhous Nixon came on a political pilgrimage not to Canterbury but to Bucharest in the summer of 1969. He was the first American president to visit a Soviet-bloc country after the war.

One million Romanians filled the streets and avenues of the capital along the motorcade's route from the Otopeni airport, which yet unfinished had been adorned for the occasion with flags, flowers, portraits of the two leaders, and colorful balloons.

Communist "sinner" Ceausescu, who badly needed "martyr" Nixon's blessings following his schism with Moscow the year before, always studied the character of foreign dignitaries. He had made a close study of Nixon before he decided to welcome him to Romania with top honors two years before, when the American was a simple citizen and a lawyer in New York. Nixon's second trip to Romania, several months after his inauguration as president, was a good diplomatic feat for Bucharest.

While Ceausescu was rolling out the red carpet, the people's enthusiasm for the American president that they cheered at the top of their lungs was hard to describe.

Pushed by the crowd, which wanted to see the "most powerful man in the world," I could hardly keep my standing spot that I had found in the morning near the *Arc de Triomphe*. The whole city was boiling with curiosity, and the police, aided by army soldiers, had a tough time keeping the enthusiastic crowds under control.

On top of the *Arc* (a faithful copy of its older brother in Paris), two big TV cameras had been fixed on tripods to broadcast live the official cavalcade. The operators who handled them looked like huge birds attempting to take off. Suddenly, sirens pierced the air, and several police cars whizzed by, checking the route and making sure that everything was fine.

A volcano of ovations came from the direction of *Casa Scanteii*, a grandiose state construction in the wedding-cake baroque style of the Stalin era, half a mile away. The crowds packing the square around the *Arc* pushed forward to get a better view. Struggling not to miss anything, I let myself be carried away by the torrent, like a boat on a stormy sea. In the human melee, somebody dropped a small American paper flag. A man leaned over quickly to pick it up. The pressure from the crowd almost wrestled him to the ground. "I'll keep it," the man said, folding the crumpled flag on its stick.

After four hours of waiting, the crowds became more agitated. Under the onslaught of the midday heat, some fashioned paper cones to cover their heads. A group of Czech tourists prepared their small cameras. Coming from the seaside, they had arrived in Bucharest before the access to the capital was blocked for security reasons. "We didn't want to miss this occasion," a young Czech said. "We came to Bucharest to see the American president. We won't see him in Prague too soon."

An army helicopter was hovering at a low altitude.

"Here he comes," shouted a middle-aged man from his vantage position on the steps leading to the *Arc*. Applause and ovations gushed out from the crowd. "That's him," hollered a woman. "I recognize his face. I saw him on TV when he was waiting for the American astronauts on the boat."

The official motorcade was slowly advancing along the Kiseleff Avenue, flanked by old chestnut trees. "This would have been hard to believe just several years ago," said a man. "It's a good thing for Romania," added somebody else. "Even a very good thing."

After several minutes the motorcade came to a sudden halt at a stone's throw from the *Arc*, because the crowds chanting "Nix-on, Nix-on, Hoo-rah, hoo-rah" and "Romania-America" had obstructed the passageway. A door opened in the black Mercedes, and Nixon jumped outside with a broad smile on his face and threw his arms upward—to the dismay of the Secret Service agents accompanying and protecting him. Enthusiastically greeted by Bucharestians, he plunged into the crowds and began to shake hands with them. Yes, he was an American president in the flesh and not a mirage!

An American president in Romania! How was it possible? Many could not believe it. Tears of joy were falling down many cheeks. What will Brezhnev say now? Won't he chew his thick eyebrows, angry with rage?

To the people, Nixon's visit had to be viewed as an expression of support for Ceausescu. The United States would come to his assistance, if necessary, to save his communist throne, still in danger of being shattered by the Russians. That's what the Romanian leaders wanted others to believe, although they were aware that the Americans didn't share their view.

In fact, Washington did not plan to involve itself in the region more than its political agenda permitted. And the Soviets knew this. Therefore, there was no danger that Romania would stride out of Moscow's sphere of influence.

The United States' prestige had reached unseen heights after the Apollo 11 space mission had landed on the moon two weeks before. Romania was the only Soviet-bloc country that broadcast live the touchdown of the lunar module and Neil Armstrong's first steps on the moon.

The moon landing had fired the Romanians' imagination to such a degree that many newborns would be named Apollo and Neil, a modest contribution that American science made to the broadening of the stock of proper names in the country.

In its most glorious moment in its history until then, the Romanian, state-controlled television kept its viewers glued to their screens by showing all the stages that led to the landing in the Sea of Tranquility.

When Armstrong uttered his famous words, millions of Romanians, with their eyes red from lack of sleep, witnessed the historic moment and greeted the breathtaking adventure of man in outer space. Many of them left for work without touching their beds, preferring to leave their homes early and wander on the streets in excitement.

It was wonderful to be a Romanian in those moments. It was fantastic to know that the president of the most industrially developed nation in the world would come to visit your small country on the eastern edge of Europe. If Chaucer came here, it would have had no influence on Romanian policy. If the Wife of Bath came, if the Reeve himself came, they could not get an audience for a public lecture on English literature. The United States and Nixon were on everybody's lips.

All my efforts to get closer to Nixon and welcome him were rendered impossible by the secret agents, both Romanian and American, who quickly formed a wall of protection around him.

If somebody wanted to assassinate Nixon, he didn't have to be a sharpshooter. But, in Romania's capital, nobody wanted to kill an American president. Nixon had descended from his Air Force One like a god, and the flock of people who greeted him looked at him with veneration.

> My angel, little angel
> That I received from God,
> I'm small, you make me tall
> I'm weak, you make me strong.

"America will defend us against the Russians and Brezhnev's doctrine of limited sovereignty," some were commenting. "Brezhnev, what the heck are you saying now?" Others were cursing the Soviet leader aloud and laughing.

"Speaking on behalf of all of the American people, I wish to express my deep appreciation for the very warm welcome that you have extended to us on this occasion, and I bring with me the warm good wishes and feelings of friendship from all of the American people to all the people of Romania," Nixon said in his arrival remarks.

Like Chaucer's portrait of The Man of Law ("The Lawyer's Tale"), who impressed the Canterbury pilgrims with his high standing and silk adorned clothes, Nixon made an impact on his Romanian hosts for the "many robes" (figuratively) he owned and for other reasons:

> Because of learning and his high renown,
> He took large fees and many robes could own.
> So great a purchaser was never known.
> All was fee simple to him, in effect,
> Wherefore his claims could never be suspect.
> Nowhere a man so busy of his class,
> And yet he seemed much busier than he was.

Not everybody in the crowd shared Romanian hosts' enthusiasm.

"Too late America, too late. History has already been written in this part of the world," said an old man who wasn't basking in the general euphoria. "Why didn't you come after Yalta," he said, spitting out the words between the free spaces left among his missing teeth.

After he shook hands with several Bucharestians, Nixon got back in the black sedan, and the motorcade resumed its triumphal progress, making a left turn behind the *Arc*. The American guest was heading for the residence reserved for him in Romania: the Elisabeta Palace on the banks of Lake Herestrau that belonged to Romania's royal family.

By now two buttons were missing from my shirt, and the human torrent pushed me in the opposite direction, dumping me on a side street.

"Too late, too late," the old man kept mumbling to himself. He spat with disgust and said, "Everything is a farce."

For him, as for other Romanians who had spent years in Stalinist jails after the war, Nixon was a clown like Roosevelt and Churchill, despised in Eastern Europe because they abandoned this part of the world without a fight for Moscow's benefit.

In a book unique in the communist world in the early 1970s, two Romanian professors would present a study of American presidents. Nixon would get high grades for ending the Vietnam War. Ironically, his presidency would be handled with kid gloves, despite the Watergate scandal that was never mentioned.[9] Later on, the Romanian state-run media would break the silence and blame his resignation on the US Congress and the media. His friend, Ceausescu, did a great job trying to keep the scandal under wraps for Romanians. A communist friend in need, is a capitalist friend indeed!

The two ambitious and acerbic politicians, united by the same contempt for the media, had something in common: a desire to hide their true faces and conduct their business with an iron hand.

That was easy for the dictator Ceausescu, the "Danube of Wisdom" as he was officially flattered, but it was more difficult for the sneaky capitalist

---

9 Camil Muresan and Alexandru Vianu, *Presedinte la Casa Alba (President at the White House)* (Bucharest: Editura Politica, 1974).

Nixon, who was labeled with derisive nicknames such as "Tricky Dick" and "Slick Rick."

Nixon already had a good impression of Romanians and their talent for dealings of all nature. When Romania's richest prewar entrepreneur, Nicolae Malaxa, asked for permanent residency in the United States after the communist takeover, a young senator of California would help him: his name—Richard Nixon, a lawyer by profession. The future American president introduced a bill in Congress in 1951 granting Malaxa permanent residency. Nixon's action was stimulated with a check (some say bribe) for $100,000, given as a contribution to his political campaign. Malaxa's "modest present," $1 million in today's dollars, is revealed in a book by Anthony Summers and other authors.[10] Though Nixon's bill was met with objections and did not pass, the future American president would step in again a bit later. Malaxa, who had business ties to Nazi Germany in Romania, would establish Western Tube Corp., a company supposed to manufacture seamless steel tubes for oil wells in Whittier, California, Nixon's hometown. The United States was embroiled in the Korean War, and oil was in great demand. In a letter in support of the scheme, Senator Nixon argued that Malaxa was critical to the success of the factory and should be a "first priority" candidate for permanent residency. What is interesting is that the address of Malaxa's ghost company, which would never produce anything, was in the same building where Nixon's law firm was located.

"I'm not a crook," Nixon would state in a press conference in 1973, amid charges related to the Watergate break-in and subsequent scandal. Perhaps he was not a crook, but was he a liar? Yes.

Both he and Ceausescu had boundless confidence in their luck. They were two wily and paranoid politicians who, despite their difference in interests, philosophy, and politics, made good friends and showed mutual respect. Like two businessmen, they knew that power and diplomacy smell equally good in East and West.

Eventually they would plant their own seeds of destruction.

---

10 Anthony Summers, *The Arrogance of Power: The Secret World of Richard Nixon* (New York: Penguin Books, 2001).

In his memoirs, Nixon would write that his visit to Romania in 1969 paved the way for the resumption of diplomatic ties with China, disclosing that Romania played a go-between role in the thawing of relations between Washington and Peking.

Ceausescu, who was a closet admirer of US foreign-policy achievements, would build a summer residence for himself at Neptun, on the Black Sea coast, that looked very much like Nixon's retreat at Key Biscayne, Florida.

In another display of admiration for the American, Ceausescu would replace his presidential plane, a Soviet-made Iliyshin-62 turboprop, with a brand-new Boeing 707. With the exception of the secret electronic equipment, it would be a faithful copy of Nixon's Air Force One.

Perhaps one day the political pundits will find an explanation for Nixon's admiration for Ceausescu, despite the latter's lack of education and dictatorial style. Perhaps Romania's mediation between the United States and China was Ceausescu's strength that impressed Nixon so much.

The American president never missed a chance to show his gratitude.

When Ceausescu returned Nixon's visit and traveled to Washington DC in October 1970—one of several visits he eventually paid to the United States—he was awarded the certificate of honorary citizenship of Disneyland, which Mickey Mouse conferred on him. According to the *New York Times*, Ceausescu "established diplomatic relations today with Mickey Mouse," becoming the first Communist head of state to visit Disneyland. After his return to Bucharest, he would proudly display the certificate, together with a photo, in his museum of the "Proofs of Love," popularly dubbed "The Ceausescus' Storehouse of Junk," showing off awards, decorations, gifts, and trinkets given to him and his wife, Elena, on their trips round the world.

The thousands of gifts and tributes in ten special halls of the National History Museum on *Calea Victoriei* included moon rocks, two captured U.S. army rifles and Congolese elephant tusks. The halls were opened for the *Conducator's* 60th birthday.

Beyond the elephant tusks were North Vietnamese contributions of the two American automatic rifles and what was said to be part of the

1,000[th] U.S. plane shot down over Bac Hai province. Across the hall were no fewer than three Romanian flags taken into space aboard American rockets, two sets of moon rocks brought back by the U.S. astronauts, a souvenir picture of Camp David and a framed portrait of the White House. Americans in the friendship force, a people-to-people program, contributed three flashlights. They were on display along with their batteries.

The Interior Ministry contributed a huge plaque of Romania dotted with oil wells, cranes, coalmines and power shovels, guarded by a gigantic policeman whose towering figure extended almost from the Soviet Union, in the north, to Bulgaria, in the south.

On the occasion of Ceausescu's sixty-fifth birthday in 1983—six years before his violent removal from power—Nixon would send his Romanian buddy such an extolling letter that one might ask if the former US president was in his right mind:

"Ever since we first met and talked together in 1967, I have followed your evolution as a statesman. Your vigor, your independent spirit, your acute intelligence, and particularly your skill in handling both internal and international problems place you in the first ranks of the world's leaders…

…I am sure that your best moments will come during your second decade as president, when you will continue the same daring and independent course you have decided upon for your people."

Ceausescu, in his turn, was strongly impressed by the modesty and "healthy social origins" of the Nixons:

"As you could see, I went with him to the (farmer's) market. He was rather devoid of the snobbery that other (leaders) suffer from although he is the president of a big country, not only capitalist, for, honestly, economically speaking, it's the biggest country in the world," Ceausescu told a Politburo meeting after the visit.

"He didn't come on the position of a big power; we went to the markets, and he shook hands with all the greengrocers," the Romanian leader commended Nixon in front of his Party pals.

And he went on, as if growing vegetables was Nixon's main business and hobby in his youth:

"It's true, he was in the greengrocer business; until he was twenty years old, he sold vegetables. From the social origin standpoint, he has a better social origin than many communists. His wife is a coal-miner's daughter."

Neither was Nixon stingy in singing Ceausescu's praises:

"It has been my privilege to visit over sixty countries in the world, and of all the countries I have visited, there has been none that has been more memorable than the visit to Romania," Nixon would say in his departure remarks.

On the side street where the torrent of people had dumped me and others, not everybody was happy.

"Actors, second-rate actors," said the old man scornfully, summing up the experience of a bitter life. Biting from a piece of bread and still cursing and mumbling, he walked away, knowing that, as Hegel said, history repeats itself twice: once as a tragedy, the second time as a farce.

The tragedy had been the occupation of this country after the war by the Red Army. The farce was the Americans' triumphal entry in Bucharest and the popular belief that they came as "liberators."

The old man was right.

As a political actor, Nixon was one of the most puzzling and tragic American presidents—and perhaps the most Shakespearean of all. He was both bigger and smaller than life, a man struggling with an inferiority complex, dominated by pathos, cynicism, resentments, hatred, and anxieties. A "cinematic creation" as somebody said. Nevertheless, he had his own merits, particularly in the foreign-policy realm where his pragmatism drew much acclaim.

As for Nixon's assertion that Ceausescu's "best moments" would come in his second decade as president, namely after 1984, that's the most foolish thing ever uttered by an American president.

Friends until the bitter end, the two would end dramatically. Nixon would be forced to resign after the Watergate scandal, and Ceausescu would be overthrown by the fury of the hungry and ill-treated masses.

Even their departures from their jobs would resemble in some way: Nixon would leave the White House in the presidential helicopter with California as his final destination as a retiree, and Ceausescu would be rescued from the rooftop of the Communist Party headquarters by a Romanian Army helicopter. After three days, he and his wife would be executed by firing squad in a hail of over forty bullets. This would happen after a show trial (with the blessing of Iliescu, who would replace him as Romania's president).

Nixon would follow Ceausescu to the immaterial world five years later.

"Long live our friendship," as Nixon said during his visit to Bucharest. "Here on earth...and beyond," one could add.

But those events were well in the future. On that day in 1969 when several thousand Romanians who wanted to see the American guest gathered anew in the afternoon in downtown Bucharest, they unfolded their paper flags carefully and began to wave them and cheer, but more subdued than in the morning.

"What are you going to do with the American flag?" I asked a man who said he was a Party member.

"I'll keep it for my son. Who knows? The wheel of history turns and turns and turns..."

## 5

*The "Associated Press" agency is interested to obtain through its correspondents data not meant for publishing.*

—NOTE FROM 3rd DIRECTORATE FOR COUNTERESPIONAGE
IN MY SECURITATE DOSSIER

Valea Carasu
Fall 1973

I am traveling with Nick Ludington, my first AP boss, who obtained the authorities' permission to open a news bureau in Romania's capital.

The office occupies one room in a sprawling, state-owned apartment covering an entire floor in a prewar elegant villa not far from the InterContinental Hotel and the US Embassy. He would live here for one year—together with his wife, Cassandra, and their preteen sons, Nicky and Max—before moving to his next assignment.

Nick is driving his brand-new sedan, a Romanian-made Dacia station wagon, on a fact-finding trip to Constanta and Tulcea for a couple of stories about the Black Sea coast and the Danube Delta.

We are crossing the Carasu Valley in Dobrogea, a limestone plain covered by thick deposits of loess and sprinkled with stony elevations. According to some, the valley might be an old riverbed of the Danube or another river that used to flow into the Danube.

We had been riding for nearly three hours after leaving Bucharest early that morning before Nick stops the car on a hillock to get something to eat. Some distance away is a slice of the abandoned Danube-Black Sea Canal, where five thousand political prisoners were said to have died while

working on its excavation. In the words of the Gheorghiu Dej communist regime in the early 1950s, the canal was supposed to be a "grave of
Romania's bourgeoisie," a vast labor camp with fourteen colonies of hard
labor, totaling tens of thousands of political prisoners.

We step out of the car, and Nick walks to the trunk and gets out a small
box with ham and cheese sandwiches, which his wife had prepared for us.
We sit on a grassy mound, several meters away from the car, and we start
eating. We are the only human souls as far as the eye can see.

I look at the vestiges of the old canal where work was abruptly stopped
after Stalin's death, and I think that now is the right moment. Here you can
be confident that there are no microphones to pick up your words.

I finish eating quickly and say, "I'd like to tell you something. I got several phone calls from the Securitate in the last few weeks, and they asked
me to meet with them and talk about you and me." Nick takes another
sandwich from the basket and doesn't appear too surprised by what I tell
him.

"I met with them a few times. They want to know who is visiting your
office apartment, especially Romanians but also foreigners. They are interested in finding out your contacts with Romanian officials and private
citizens, and they want me to inform them about your movements. I didn't
tell you about this until now because we met only in your office where our
conversations are picked up by the bugs in the walls, no doubt."

Nick smiles. "I'm not surprised they want to know this," he says.

"I didn't know what to do," I continue. "I was expecting their call, but
I felt intimidated. It's not because of my lack of courage; it's my lack of
experience in dealing with these guys. I should have refused to meet with
them and hung up the phone," I added. "Now I regret it."

After a brief pause, I went on. "You can fire me if you want, but if you
hire somebody else, that person will also be contacted by the Securitate
and urged to report on your activities."

I stand up abruptly. I pick up a little stone from the ground, and I toss
it as far as I can. I am so tense I feel I will explode if I don't do something
physically.

"I appreciate your honesty. Our embassy people told me how things are here. Actually, I learned about this before my arrival to Romania," he says. An English-language newspaper in Turkey had employed Nick before AP in Ankara hired him.

"I have no reasons to fire you. I met your former chief at Radio Bucharest at a reception, and we talked about you and your work. I know who you are, and it was my choice to hire you as my assistant. If I asked the authorities for a replacement, I'd not know anything about the person they'd send me," he says, finishing eating and opening a can of Tuborg beer.

"So you can do as you want. I don't know how long I'll stay here—a year, two years, maybe three. Then I'll get another assignment in a different part of the world. But you will remain here. I don't want to make any problems for you."

"You hired me to translate newspaper articles, answer phone calls, schedule appointments with Romanian officials, accompany you as a translator, and send your stories by teleprinter," I reply. "Don't invite me to family parties. I don't want to meet with anybody outside your office. The less I know, the better for me. I'll tell them that I know nothing, and they'll believe me because those whom you meet will be watched closely, including myself. I prefer that they know all my movements not from me but from the others."

Nick starts laughing. "OK, if that helps you in any way. You do as you want. If they want you to meet with them, fine, as far as I am concerned. I don't have anything to hide, and even if I did, they wouldn't be able to know and neither would you."

"I'll be acquiring experience in dealing with them. Perhaps it will help me in the future," I answer.

It turned out I was right. My "apprenticeship" with the Securitate organs would be very useful for me, although they would create greater problems when I would be alone at the office after Nick's departure.

I feel relieved. I am thinking, "This way, I can play dumb without raising their suspicions." And that's exactly what I did.

Once I met with a Securitate officer in his car. He flashed a dozen invitation cards to a party at the US Embassy before my eyes. How he got them, I had no idea. He said: "You want to go there? To meet foreigners? To tell them who you are and what you do?"

I said, "No, I'm not interested; to hell with all diplomats. They tell you lies."

He started laughing and said, "That's true, but you can help us if you learn something interesting."

"No," I said, "I don't give a damn. I don't think I can have an intelligent conversation with diplomats, and I don't want to waste my time."

He looked at me in disbelief. He was probably thinking that I was crazy or stupid or both. He didn't know what to think. I doubt that any-body had answered him in such a way. He flashed the pile of invitations at me again. I refused him anew. I was thinking, "This is another way to control and turn me into an informer." The more contacts you had with foreign citizens, the more suspicious you became in the Securitate's eyes…and the more you felt compelled to tell them about your rela-tions so that they become less suspicious. It was a classical catch-22 situation.

"Let me tell you something else," he said, seeing that I was not the pliable person the Securitate thought I was. "For us, you're 'Udrea.' That's the rule. Nobody uses his actual name. Your family name starts with a 'U,' so you'll be known in your doings for us as Udrea."

"Holy hell!," I thought. These guys do take my activity as an "inform-er" seriously, and not only that, they change my name as well. Who knew what I was getting into and how I should play this game. They wouldn't get anything of substance from me, anyway.

Aloud, I said, "And if your name is Popescu, what's your code name? How many proper names start with a "P"? I started declaiming: Pandele, Pepelea, Pintilie, Pahontu, Panduru, Pacala, Petre, Panait, Pancu, Petcu, Piticu…" I realized that there are a lot, perhaps several hundred—hundreds of potential informers whose names start with "P." Communist Romania never had a problem with proper names. Among the Soviet-bloc countries, only East Germany's *Stasi* had more officers and informers than Romania's Securitate.

After two or three months, I got a phone call at home, and one of the "organs" said that he wanted to meet with me at *Piata Romana*. When I arrived, we shook hands, and he asked me to come with him to an apartment building across from the Magheru movie theater. We entered a small and sparsely furnished apartment that reeked of cheap cigarette smoke. It was one of the Securitate secret houses where they met with their sources.

He asked me to sit down, and he showed me a sheet of paper on which was written in block letters *ANGAJAMENT*. "Read it," the officer said. I read it. It was a formal pledge of collaboration with the Securitate. "Sign it down in the left-hand corner."

"I don't think I'm going to do this," I told myself. But I said aloud, "What do you need my signature for? If you want to talk to me, you telephone me, and we meet downtown like we did today."

"Yeah," he said, "but we have to make this official. Suppose this American reporter you're working for also works for the CIA. He was in Turkey before coming here." (They knew that Kirschen also worked in Turkey for London newspapers during the war). "We know that he uses only a part of the data he obtains as a press correspondent in his stories. The rest is used for other purposes. Perhaps he shares this information with the embassy or with other people."

He tried to impress or scare me, without doubt. What he said was utterly stupid. "If the information comes from official sources, why does it matter how or how much of it is being used?" I asked. "We talk to various government officials. Last month we met with officials from the State Planning Committee to discuss economic issues, for example. I am sure that no state secrets were divulged by them on this occasion."

Each time we went to meet with officials, there were at least two or three people around, one of whom was taking notes of the things that were discussed. The scribe was the Securitate hand in the respective institution, and he never introduced himself to visitors.

My Securitate debater looked at me in a different way and didn't comment. "It would be better for you to sign it. It's for your own good," he said.

"I'm sorry," I answered, "but I don't see why I should sign this agreement."

"We want you to be more active. The information you have given us until now was not too useful for us. You should get involved more. There are things you're hiding from us. You could get into trouble if he was sent here with a different mission than that of a journalist. This guy is very skilled. He knows what and how to ask to get what he wants."

I didn't give in. "It's not my business to play the detective. I was hired as a secretary and translator."

"Sign it," he barked authoritatively.

I read the text of the pledge once again, and I told him that I didn't see why I should do that. "Why are you hesitating," he said. "It means that you are not a good Romanian."

"I'm not a good Romanian? I don't think we should continue this discussion," I said. I stood up abruptly and I headed for the door of the apartment. I unlocked it, and I got out.

At the bus stop, I thought that my reaction was perhaps exaggerated, and I wiped my palms as I noticed the cold sweat on my entire body. Perhaps it would have been better to continue talking to this "organ," to explain myself and to mollify him. But I had lost my patience when he became so insistent and because he said that I wasn't a "good Romanian" if I didn't put my signature on that written agreement. *He* was a good Romanian, at least. If that's how a good Romanian should behave, so be it. Don't count on me, comrades.

It was the last time I saw him, and the only time when I was asked to sign the pledge. Perhaps they realized that I did not take my contacts with them seriously and that it was more of a cat-and-mouse game on my part. I think that this made them extremely suspicious of me, but they would wait patiently to see how things would end for me. They assumed that time was not on my side. (Actually it wouldn't be on *their* side).

Many years after this episode, when I saw my dossier at the National Council for the Study of the Securitate Archives, I found attached the *ANGAJAMENT* page that I refused to sign. I read the comment from the officer I met on that occasion: "The pledge was shown to him, which he read but did not sign." I am happy I hadn't let myself be intimidated, although when this happened I had serious concerns about how things would evolve in the future.

Leafing through my dossier, I come across a Securitate report dated May 1984. I apologize for the *langue du bois* used by the authorities. Here it is verbatim, in its entirety and posthumous glory:

*Ministerul de Interne*                                           *Strict secret*
*Departamentul Securitatii Statului*                     *Exemplar unic*
*Directia a III-a*

### REPORT
*with proposals to abandon informer "UDREA"*

*He was recruited as an informer on 20.09.1973 to supply us directly with information from his work place, exercise an informative control over the AP correspondents who come to our country and for his use near American diplomats, first of all the press attaché.*

*In the process of collaboration with the Securitate organs, "UDREA" has furnished a reduced number of data [and] has shown a permanent reticence in his contacts with us, demonstrating with premeditation lack of consistency, operativity, and opportunity in his informations.*

*Although we tried several times to spur him in his activity of gathering and supplying us with facts from his field of activity, including his use for achieving concrete tasks vis-à-vis some American diplomats, "UDREA" has mentioned the "professional secret" which he must observe and the fact that he does not have relations with American diplomats or other foreign citizens, an assertion without merit in reality.*

*Aspects of insincerity and disinformation in his attitude toward the Securitate organs have also appeared in connection with his brother's illegal settling abroad about which he never informed us, although this happened two years ago.*

*At the same time, through special means, it was established that "UDREA" plans to settle illegally in the United States of America, in which sense, through a personal arrangement, he has planned a trip "in the interest of service" to that country.*

*"UDREA" has a difficult character, being dominated by his desire to prosper materially, and he shows hostility toward RS Romania in his press reports that he publishes through AP.*

*Taking all this into consideration WE PROPOSE:*

*- to get the approval for abandoning informer "UDREA"…*

*Approved: Chief of service Lt. Col. Gheorghe Diaconescu*

*[In Diaconescu's handwriting, in the upper left-hand corner, was this notation: "Must achieve a systematic control of the contents of news circulating on the wires of AP agency."]*

Reading all this gibberish, I am shrieking with laughter. My, oh, my, I'm looking better in my own eyes. Just imagine telling the Securitate about the "professional secret" a press correspondent has to stick to in his dealings with the political police in order to protect his sources. They must have thought that I was somewhat eccentric, if not altogether foolish! As for their plans to make me report on US diplomats, during my fourteen years as an AP reporter in Bucharest, I'm not sure if I went to the embassy more than three or four times. Knowing what happened to Kirschen, I stayed away from diplomats as much as possible, with the exception of Fourth of July celebrations and press conferences.

For the authorities, reporting about Romania's problems truthfully was an act of treason, as they were going from bad to worse. I noticed that Diaconescu had kept me under continuous surveillance since 1973. At the beginning he was a Securitate captain, but eleven years later, when I was accused of being hostile to the regime and was abandoned as an "informer," Diaconescu would be promoted to the rank of colonel. Who knows how many lives he ruined in the process. He tried his best with me but without success. Frankly, I don't know why he waited so long to drop me as an "informer" when he should have done this the moment I refused to sign the *ANGAJAMENT.* They should have realized much sooner that I never took my dialogue with them seriously.

As far as I was concerned, I was certainly a distinct case through what I was doing. AP was the only Western news agency that had a permanent office in Bucharest, and I was the only Romanian working there. After Nick Ludington's departure to Beirut, I would become a correspondent—a position that no other Romanian would have during Ceausescu's "Golden Epoch."

It was a mystery to the authorities why AP alone had a bureau in Romania—why not Reuters or France Presse or the other US news agency, United Press International? For the Securitate the activity of news gathering and reporting was simply an excuse, a smoke screen to hide the "real objective": spying. Their thinking had not changed at all along the years. They knew from Kirschen, who was the most active foreign correspondent in Bucharest in the late 1940s, that over 80 per cent of the news coming from Romania was carried by the Associated Press, about the same percentage that was now. What was their explanation for that? To justify their mission and methods, and to placate their delusional paranoia, the Securitate needed to continually uncover spies, traitors, and enemies. Journalists doing their job were a good target for them, as the regime considered free, objective reportage a criminal anti-state activity—only, this time, they could not extract "confessions" under physical torture.

\* \* \*

I often think of the time when I was Nick Ludington's assistant. It's interesting how I met him. First, I should be grateful to Catinca Ralea. She hired me as a reporter in the English Department of the state-run Radio Bucharest in 1971, where she was an editor, at a time when I had no idea where to go and what to do. I was laid off about two years later when the institution was "reorganized" and downsized, and those who were not Communist Party members and didn't want to join, like me, were shown the green light. My father was the editor-in-chief of a technical publication for more than twenty years, and although he was repeatedly asked to join the Party throughout the years, he diplomatically delayed a decision until he retired. Before she had to fire me and others, conforming to orders from above, Catinca gave me the tip about the American reporter who had gotten permission to open the AP bureau in Bucharest and who was looking for an assistant. She had good ties to US diplomats. Her father, Mihai Ralea, a cultural personality with leftist views, was Romania's ambassador to Washington after the war. Petru Groza's procommunist government named him to that position.

That's how I met Nick. He hired me, although the Romanian authorities didn't seem too pleased by his choice. They would have preferred to place their own man, but they didn't want to greet the American correspondent with a refusal from the beginning. After his promotion to chief of Middle East Services in Beirut, Nick left Romania one year later, and I became the AP's sole hand in Romania.

That was my professional story, in a nutshell.

Transitioning from the language of literature and literary criticism that I had become familiar with at the University to the language of American journalism was a tough move for me. Good-bye Shakespeare, James Joyce, D. H. Lawrence, and all the others. This was a different language that I had to learn, with new words and phrases in the spheres of economy, politics, and sports that I had never heard before. I was more familiar with Chaucer's Middle English than with American English. I knew something from my two years as a radio reporter, but it was too little.

I soon realized that English is the language of journalism in the same way that French is so fit for poetry, Italian for singing, and German for rendering abstract notions, i.e., philosophy.

English is "economical," analytical, and very nimble and graphic, a perfect vehicle for news story writing where one is limited to a certain number of words and typographic space is at a premium. If a 200-word story is translated from English into Romanian, French, or any other language, about 220 words would be needed for the same text—a 10 per cent increase. Besides, most of the words in the daily English vocabulary are one-syllable words.

Rene J. Cappon—a former news editor and writing coach who was born in Vienna and for whom English was his third language, after German and Hungarian—was the author of the much-appreciated *AP Guide to Good Writing*. He would often meditate aloud about "the mystery of the English language, the magic that makes certain combinations of words fit together, like notes in a musical score, while the same words in other [foreign-language] combinations jar."

Word combinations like die-hard, high-rise, high-tech, fast-paced, slow-motion, trigger-happy, action-packed, gun-shy, smoke-free, nail-biting, all-inclusive, ill-advised, and others are found only in English and can't be translated into other languages by using two equivalent words. Most often, they are written in English as readers in most languages have become familiar with the English terms.

Trying to brush up my "journalistic" English, I started reading the only English-language publications available on the market: *The Morning Star*, the British Communist Party daily, and *The Moscow Times*. I was, no doubt, one of the most diligent readers of the two publications, scanning absolutely everything, including the weather forecasts. In a short time, I became an expert on the "ardent desire of the socialist countries, headed by the Soviet Union, for peace," and "the struggle for national liberation of African countries." I also knew lots of details about the "miners' strikes for higher salaries in Wales," as well as the "failure of US imperialism in Indochina," not to mention the topic of the "brave civil rights activist Angela Davis" who was famous throughout the communist world.

I could very well apply for a job with *Pravda* or *TASS* news agency in Moscow.

I learned American journalism the hard way.

One day I received a telex message from Vienna, saying that Rtr carried a story about rumors according to which tennis ace Ilie Nastase had divorced his Belgian fashion model wife, Dominique. I asked jokingly if Rtr did not stand for Radio Transylvania? "No, moron, that's an acronym for Reuters news agency, man, don't you know even that?" No, honestly, I didn't. But I knew in compensation to recite Hamlet's famed soliloquy and how many sonnets Shakespeare wrote, or how many times Lady Chatterley's gamekeeper screwed her, and what kind of rifles Hemingway used on his African safaris.

Working with Nick was a schooling in courage for me. For the first time, I saw that somebody could tell the truth about Ceausescu's Romania, and I was so proud! Nick wrote the stories, and I punched tape to send them by telex to Vienna or London, but while I was doing this, I often became fearful. Working with this man, whom I admired so much, could send me to jail. What Romanian reporter would dare to write such stories? I thought that they would get me after he left the country, but what could I do? It was true that I didn't write the stuff, but I was his assistant. I kept him informed about the situation in the country, politically and economically, and I explained and gave him all the details and background he needed. What would happen to me after his departure?

While Nick wrote the political stories, in his absence from the country I started to report on sports (mainly tennis and soccer) and US-Romanian cultural activities. From the beginning I was amazed by the trust Nick and the AP put in me. I was not used to this. At the Radio, nobody trusted anybody. The totalitarian system treated reporters like potential criminals. Every story was checked, double checked and triple checked for political correctness, and only after the "clear head" gave his approval was the story made public.

I recall the stories he wrote about the stifling bureaucracy, the lack of freedoms, and the consolidation of Ceausescu's personal power. Other stories were about Romania's dubious independence from Moscow, though it was the only Soviet-bloc country that had diplomatic ties with Israel and West Germany. It also refused to join the other "brotherly" countries in their invasion of Czechoslovakia. Did this make it a democratic country?

One of Nick's scoops, which got widespread play in the Western media, was about the resignation of I. G. Maurer as Romania's premier in 1974 after he was censured for his stand on Romania's forced industrialization that Ceausescu unconditionally supported. His resignation opened the way for Ceausescu to strengthen his control over the Communist Party and the government. Maurer's departure was a crushing blow to those who wanted to curb Ceausescu's élan to become Romania's "Dear Leader." From now on he would lead the country unopposed and with an iron hand.

Ceausescu's main reason for sending Maurer into retirement was to grab the newly created post of president of Romania. On that occasion Salvador Dali sent him a telegram that was published in *Scanteia* (Spark), the Communist Party organ, on April 4, 1974. It read, "I deeply appreciate your historic act to create the presidential scepter." Splashed on the first page was a photo showing Stefan Voitec, the head of parliament, handing Ceausescu the "presidential silver scepter" after taking the oath of office.

We laughed until we felt like our sides would split when I translated Dali's telegram, which Nick mentioned in his story. Ceausescu was the "royal" president of a communist country! Romanians were surprised that such a thing was published in the Party newspaper. After all, Dali, with sarcasm and irony, was making fun of the *Conducator* (the Romanian word for *Fuehrer*), but the authorities took the eccentric surrealist painter seriously!

I still remember the beginning of the 500-word story, which I typed on the telex machine before sending it to our Vienna bureau:

BUCHAREST, Romania (AP) - Nicolae Ceausescu, already the most absolute among East Europe's absolute leaders, emerged with an even firmer grip on power in Romania, after a major reshuffle of personnel and functions. The 55-year-old Ceausescu, first secretary of the Romanian Communist Party and titular head of state as chairman of the State Council, will be named "President of the Socialist Republic of Romania," a new post.

Punching tape, I felt butterflies in my stomach. I was frightened. Calling him "the most absolute among East Europe's absolute leaders" was something that Romanians were afraid to say aloud, let alone write in a story, though most of them agreed to that description. At Radio Bucharest where I worked before, I would have been arrested in less than an hour.

After he finished the story, Nick got on his car and sped off to attend a press conference. Left alone, I went to the bathroom and I washed my face with cold water. I saw a tube of Colgate toothpaste, I squeezed a small amount in the palm of my hand and I swallowed it. Passing through the living room on my way back to the office, I poured half a glass of Cutty Sark whisky and I finished it in one gulp. After the toothpaste, the whisky had a queer taste.

"This is not going to end well for me. No, no," I thought. "And this is just the beginning. They'll get me, sooner or later."

The story carried Nick's byline but the Securitate already considered me an accomplice who made him familiar with the workings of the system. But I was so proud because Nick was able to tell the world the story of Ceausescu's self-aggrandizement plans.

I was not only an accomplice, but also a thief. I found a note in my Securitate dossier from the uniformed police in which they described me as the main suspect in a burglary at the Ludingtons' apartment-office. In 1974, when Nick was touring the Middle East to report on the oil crisis, and his wife, Cassandra, was with the boys at the American Villa in the alpine resort of Sinaia, "thieves" broke into their apartment in Bucharest one night and stole all the electronic appliances they found there. Among the articles that disappeared were two tape recorders, two cameras, a dictaphone, a small transistor radio and a bulky Zenith Trans-Oceanic portable AM/FM/SW receiver that was sitting on a small table by Nick's office desk. This radio was a wonder of technology for that time: it had eleven reception bands, including marine, aviation, and weather VHF channels and frequencies. It also had a lighted map compartment and a 55-inch telescopic antenna.

In the end, the police blamed a teenager who lived in the basement of the building for stealing these articles. But as I saw that nothing happened to him and that he continued to walk freely, I had a strong suspicion that the police themselves staged the theft. They probably were intrigued by the Zenith shortwave receiver and wanted to check its inside to see if it did not hide a secret system of communication of the James Bond kind. Proof of that is the fact that when the radio was returned to Nick, together with the other stolen items, it did not operate normally, although it had been in good condition before. The Securitate must have dismantled it piece by piece to look for some emission-reception secret equipment, but when they tried to put everything back, they failed miserably. The impressive Zenith Trans-Oceanic Royal D7000Y was able to catch only a handful of stations in Europe, including the state-run Radio Bucharest! The rest were noises usually referred to as static.

To underscore the problems of Romanians' everyday life, Nick sometimes made use of quotes from the regime-controlled press or the humor of cartoonists, who were still permitted to decry some of the general shortcomings. Usually the authorities blamed incompetent local bureaucrats or inept officials—not the Party's plans of forced industrialization, the real culprit causing the Romanians' hard life.

Illustrating a story about food shortages, a cartoon published in the government paper *Romania Libera* showed a husband complaining to his wife while she served him dinner: "Tuesday, spinach…Wednesday, spinach…yesterday, spinach…today, spinach…what am I…Popeye?" In another cartoon a tourist goes to a restaurant and sees the daily menu posted outside on the door: First course—Soup. Second course—Food. Third course—Dessert.

With the best Romanian products being exported for hard currency, consumer sacrifices became the subject of countless jokes and sometimes even published humor.

Another newspaper cartoon triggered gales of laughter. It showed a theater director shouting at an actor during rehearsal:" No, no. It won't do. You must show real despair, real hopelessness, imagine for instance that you have gone out shopping for soda water."

Three years before, Ceausescu had initiated Romania's "minicultural revolution" after visits to China and North Korea and launched a neo-Stalinist offensive against cultural autonomy and attacks on noncompliant intellectuals. Interestingly, the debut of Romania's version of Mao's "cultural revolution" coincided with the debut of Ceausescu's personality cult, which would be worthy of ridicule and become the butt of jokes from 1980 until his overthrow in 1989, a period known as the "satanic decade."

Given the worsening situation, Nick and I were sometimes surprised to find out that the state censorship could be "tricked" (or let itself be tricked deliberately) by the cultural personalities of the time.

We went together to see *Hamlet* at the Nottara Theatre under the direction of Dinu Cernescu. We realized that its staging was a parable of the police state that Romania was then: "Something is rotten in the state of Denmark" was moved into the opening scene. There were mirrors everywhere enabling members of the audience to watch the movements of the characters off stage, and there was a general atmosphere of suspicion—everybody watching everybody—a direct hint to the omnipresent Securitate. Hamlet's Denmark was, in fact, Ceausescu's Romania: a political prison with bars at the windows, thick metal doors that closed with a sinister noise, narrow corridors filled with whispers. It was a repressive system that was meant to protect the "king." And the king's court was brimming with watchers and minders dressed in black, the same as Ceausescu's "court."

The play ended with the installation on the throne of Fortinbras, a Norwegian prince who initially wanted to attack Denmark. Sitting on the throne, the uncouth and ill-mannered warrior utters the last words of the play by warning the audience: "The rest is *si-len-ce*." (In the original version, these words are spoken by Hamlet before his death). Director Cernescu's artistic revision was a clear allusion to the "Soviet danger": if you want a change, it's preferable to be led by a native leader than to fall under the boot of a churlish foreigner. A native tyrant, who allows you to grumble and laugh, is still better than a foreign dictator who forces you to keep your mouth shut, without a murmur. No matter how bad the *Conducator* was, he was still better than somebody placed on the throne by Moscow, as had happened in Czechoslovakia. Perhaps this "ingenious" message made it possible for the play to pass the censor's office.

Nick wrote a cultural story focusing on this play and showing that the liberalization in arts and culture that flourished in the late '60s was about to end. There were unmistakable signs that Romanians' situation would worsen. After a few years of cultural and political liberalization that followed the "Prague Spring," a frozen wind would herald the start of the ideological winter that was to come soon. Few believed that everything would end so quickly, in a rapid twist of history.

The West still didn't know what to think. What was Romania's real face—the one before 1971 or the other after Ceausescu's cultural revolution?

For one thing, the ties with the United States were developing, having a positive impact on people's life. A Pepsi-Cola factory opened in Constanta in 1967, and for the first time, Romanians were able to taste what before had been labeled a "bourgeois concoction."

A year later Bucharest played host to the first students' bar and club, equipped with electromechanical games and billiards tables, where the atmosphere was quasi Western. Modern American art, so despised in the years of socialist realism in the 1950s, was appraised more favorably. An exhibition called "American Paintings Since 1945" opened in 1969, exhibiting works by artists of abstract expressionism and pop art such as Jackson Pollock, Robert Rauschenberg, and James Rosenquist. Several months later, Nixon's visit followed the opening.

Was Romania the "fissure" in the Soviet wall? Dubcek's Czechoslovakia was not, and neither were Catholic Poland nor Hungary, the West's spoiled child. How about Romania? To find an answer, the AP's management in New York had decided to open a bureau in Bucharest. From a distance, Romania appeared more interesting than from close proximity.

One day Nick told me that his superiors had decided to promote him as chief of Middle East Services and transfer him to Beirut. The Mideast had become an essential juncture of events and a hot zone for news after the 1973 Arab-Israeli war followed by the oil embargo of the Organization of Petroleum Exporting Countries against the United States.

And so I would become AP's sole hand in Romania. President and General Manager Wes Gallagher's letter to the Ministry of Foreign Affairs asked that they certify me as an AP correspondent as "we are confident that his services on our behalf would enable us to make certain that all essential news is covered out of Romania.

"We are hopeful that you will accredit Mr. Urma as an Associated Press representative and that he will receive any necessary assistance. He would have an AP office in his home."

That did not sit at all well with the authorities. For one thing, an American correspondent in Bucharest was viewed with more consideration than a native one. Secondly, it was the first time a Romanian would write and send stories to a Western news agency since 1950, when Kirschen was arrested. Apart from that, Gallagher's request for permission that I have a small news office in a room at home would give them unbearable headaches.

The most difficult and risky chapter of my life was about to start.

## 6

*The CIA uses in its gathering data activity press
correspondents accredited in our country*

—Dossier note from 3rd Directorate of
Counterintelligence

Bucharest
Summer 1975

After Nick Ludington's departure, my situation was uncertain. The authorities were refusing to accredit me as a correspondent, which would have allowed me to write and send stories about Romania. Nobody dared to take the responsibility for approving such a thing.

I was calling Foreign Ministry officials almost every week to ask if they had anything new. "Your Excellency, we don't have any news in this regard," Nicolae Nicoara, a third secretary in the Press and Culture Department, would tell me. That's how he addressed me, "Your Excellency," a title that was amusing and witty to him. When I heard the derision in his voice, I could hardly stop myself from responding, "Screw you, Your Highness."

Finally, one day he told me that Stefan Andrei had decided that "allowing a Romanian to work as a correspondent was not a good idea." Andrei was a Central Committee secretary in charge of international relations for the Communist Party, before he became Romania's foreign minister. So AP management's request for my accreditation had reached a high level of communist bureaucracy, and it stopped there after getting a negative response.

I decided to write Ceausescu a letter to inform him personally about my situation. On two pages, in the most respectful way, I told him why it was good for Romania to have an American news bureau in Bucharest, which played host at that time to no fewer than eleven Soviet correspondents (and KGB agents, without doubt) from various Soviet newspapers and news agencies. I complimented Ceausescu for his efforts to stop the "Stalinist abuses and illegalities" of the 1950s and for opening a more "democratic" era in the country. Then I referred to the ten years that Kirschen had spent in the Stalinist prisons of the time on trumped-up charges of espionage. Now, in the "new" Romania, such things were not possible. Therefore, to meet the interest with which the country was viewed internationally, it would be appropriate for the authorities to give me the green light to work as a correspondent. I handed the letter to a Central Committee low-level official, and I waited.

I knew that I wouldn't get an answer, but I wrote that letter for two reasons. I wanted to have something at hand if the Securitate took me to task. I was all by myself, and although the teleprinter had been installed in a small room in my parents' house, I seldom used it because of my uncertain situation. I was still being paid a full salary from AP's account at the Romanian Bank for Foreign Trade.

Secondly, sending a telex message to Vienna to let them know about my letter to Ceausescu, I deliberately alerted the "organs" which were intercepting the telex traffic going in and out of Romania. Knowing what I did, they would be less inclined to grab me while waiting for a resolution of my case from the government. I gave a copy of my letter to my father to keep in a safe place.

And that's exactly what happened. The Securitate waited to see how things would play out and didn't bother me at all during that time. However, I was certain that they were watching me.

One day, "His Excellency" Nicolae Nicoara called me to say that deputy foreign minister Vasile Gliga wanted to see me. Hey, I told myself, my letter to Ceausescu wasn't left unanswered after all. I met him in his elegant office at *Palatul Victoria*, and my heart was pumping to get out of my chest. Gliga, a career diplomat with the air of a gentleman, told me that I could work as an assistant. This was great news! When I asked him if I had permission to write and send stories, he said no. I was flabbergasted. What was I supposed to do? Clip articles from Romanian newspapers and translate them into English? Parrot what the state-run news agency, Agerpres, was saying? Our editors in Vienna were already getting their stuff. It was ridiculous. I left more concerned than when I arrived.

I wrote a letter to the chief of the Central and East European bureau in Frankfurt, describing my situation, and until the summer of 1975 I stopped sending out stories. That was one of the toughest periods in my life. I was plunging into the unknown, and, honestly, I was scared.

Years later, I'll see the letter in my Securitate dossier. Like scores of other letters to and from my brother in the United States, it had been intercepted, opened, and translated into Romanian. UM0647 was a special unit for the interception of written correspondence. (UM stands for *unitate militara*.) Here is the gist of it:

NOTE

*UM0647*
*January 1975*

*A Foreign Ministry official requested that I remove the telex from the house. "Who gave you permission to have a teleprinter and send stories?" he said. "You don't have the approval to work as a correspondent. Nor can you work as an assistant, for you can't be the assistant of somebody who doesn't even exist [...]"*

*I was told that the answer will probably be negative because I am the first Romanian who would work as a correspondent for a Western news agency after the war, and there's no precedent [...]*

The official I quoted was "His Excellency" Nicolae Nicoara, the third-class diplomat. Things were even worse than before I met with Gliga.

But, eventually, two events worked in my favor.

One day I received a call from Florian Borz, a first secretary in the Press and Culture Department, asking me to come and meet him. Once I got there, he asked me why "my American friends" insisted that I work for them. (The AP General Manager Wes Gallagher, meanwhile, had sent a second letter to the Foreign Ministry asking why it was taking so long to reach a decision and reiterating his request that they authorize me to work as a correspondent.)

"You know what?" Borz said. He had a big, round head like a pumpkin—a pumpkin with a mustache. "I don't think you have the necessary training to do that. There are Romanian journalists better prepared for a job like this."

I raised my shoulders without saying anything. "It's not you who is supposed to pick up and choose," I was thinking.

"Are you Jewish?" he asked suddenly, knowing that Kirschen, my predecessor, was Jewish. "No," I said, "I'm a Romanian Christian. There were two Orthodox monks in our family. One of them carved wood icons; the other was in charge of the printing press at the Neamt Monastery."

I thought his question was stupid. It was not possible for them not to know these details about my family.

"Can you write your autobiography for us?" he asked.

"Sure, no problem."

As we left the meeting room at the Foreign Ministry, which was probably infested with "bugs" and other surveillance devices, he accompanied me to the main exit and said, "You don't want to give up your plans, do you?"

"No, why should I?"

And all of a sudden, he said with a smile, "Your situation might get resolved. We'll let you know." We shook hands and departed.

Our conversation took place in June. At the end of July, he called me again and said, "Come to see us. We've got news for you."

He received me cordially. "You got the approval to work for AP."

I was still doubtful. "You mean I can write stories for them?"

"Yes, you can start writing stories, but be careful what you write and how you write," he said, winking an eye at me. It was more of a friendly warning than a signal of affection.

After a few days, I got a phone call from the Foreign Press Club. "Come and pick up your invitation for President Ford's visit. You have access to the airport for his arrival and the press center at the InterContinental Hotel," the caller said.

"Aha," I told myself. This was the explanation for their decision: Ford's visit to Romania in early August, right after the Conference for Security and Cooperation in Europe, where thirty-five heads of state had signed the "final act" at Helsinki.

Shortly before the Conference, the US Congress had ratified the trade agreement that included the approval of the most-favored nation status in trade with Romania, greatly expanding the bilateral relations in all fields. However, while Ceausescu was primarily concerned with developing economic, commercial, and technological ties—including nuclear energy—the United States still hoped to see Romania's government becoming closer to Western democracies.

The West's perception about Ceausescu's "liberalism" would be a great disappointment. The fake liberalization would come to a crushing halt in the following years, the effects totally contradicting the initial hopes. No, he won't be a Trojan horse but a totalitarian bully.

Six years after Nixon's groundbreaking visit, Ford's visit didn't raise too much interest among the Romanians. In their talks, Ford and Ceausescu agreed to resolve "several humanitarian issues" and act in the field of "human rights."

Forty years later, I'll see in my dossier an "informative note" written by the Securitate in which it is noted that my permission to work as an AP "assistant representative" was given with the approval of the Ministry of Foreign Affairs represented by Florian Borz, on September 5, 1975, but "without the approval of the Interior Ministry" (i.e., the Securitate). Lucky me. I'm not sure I would ever have gotten their accord.

Poor Borz. He died in the late 1970s of a heart attack. It's very improbable that the approval came from him. It must have come from higher circles in the Party or government, but they used him to cover their backs. They took precautionary measures to protect themselves if things didn't go well (and they didn't!).

After my official approval, the last thing I had to do was to remove the teleprinter from home and take it to the new office, a studio apartment in a state-owned building that housed foreign diplomats.

Thumbing through my dossier, I came across a note dated August 8, 1975, written by the 3rd Directorate (Counterintelligence).

*Measures will be taken that before the studio is assigned as an AP office, we shall introduce the ACH technique in the room. This way we'll be able to control the activity of American correspondents when they are in Bucharest and also the possibility to check on "UDREA" [i.e., URMA] permanently.*

*Captain Ilie Gheorghe*

Not so smart, dimwits! Killing two birds with one stone? You were bugging the office to listen to what the visiting AP staffers and I were talking about? What did you learn? Did you broaden your cultural and political horizons? Did you become smarter after so much listening? How many "listeners" did the Securitate have? Thousands upon thousands upon thousands, probably.

ACH was the Romanian acronym for *ascultare camere hotel,* or "hotel rooms eavesdropping"—which meant bugs everywhere: in the walls, under the floor, in the bathroom, and in the couch. It differed from the less intrusive ACT (listening to phone conversations), or ATS ("special phone listening," whatever that means). We all knew that the office would be heavily bugged. Thanks, Securitate, for your hard work and perseverance.

A month later, on September 23, 1975, another *note-report* from the same captain Ilie Gheorghe, an indefatigable prick and a "specialist officer" in eavesdropping techniques, said:

*Through ODCD [the state-run house rental agency] we will make sure that the bureau of the "Associated Press" agency in Bucharest will be located in a studio adequate from the operational standpoint in which we will introduce the ACH technique. This thing is necessary because from the information we obtained, the CIA uses in its gathering-data activity press correspondents accredited in our country.*

Did you bug the news offices of the eleven Soviet correspondents from TASS, Novosti, Pravda, Izvestia, Trud, and so on?

Reading all of this baloney, I thought, "Why not, comrades? You can introduce your ACH technique not only in the AP office in Bucharest but also in your asses, if it helps you to get valuable information. Good luck!"

Intercepting phone calls at the office or home was tormenting them day and night. Here is another *note-request* written by the 3rd Directorate officers. It's dated November 16, 1984:

*We demand the carrying out and exploitation of ICT [interceptari comunicatii telefonice] type for URMA VIOREL ("UDREA") whose profession and specialty is correspondent of "Associated Press" phone no. 116599. We're especially interested in the following problems: the control of conversations between "UDREA" and Larry Gerber, the chief of AP bureau in Vienna and the calls they'll make from that phone number, the comments and judgments they'll make and send overseas, [and] the contacts they'll establish with US or other foreign diplomats in Bucharest.*

As part of Securitate's "Plan of Measures" for the "clarification of suspicions of treason in favor of the American information service" and "my slandering and removal" from my AP job, there was measure no. 10. It called for "the surveillance of (Urma) and the use of special means of IDEB type to ensure the control of discussions he has outside the office with foreign reporters, especially during political events and visits to our country by other correspondents of the Associated Press Agency."

Measure no. 7 said: "Together with Col. Orban Moise of Independent Service 'D' we will analyze and determine the way of action for the denigration of [URMA] in his relations with other foreign reporters and with the management of the Associated Press Agency."

IDEB was an acronym for "Interception of Discussions by means of Battery-powered Emitters." Therefore, when you went to a restaurant, there were microphones planted in ashtrays, saltcellars, or buried in the table…or in the toilet bowl.

Oh my, oh my! Mr. Orban! What a pleasure. What a surprise Mr. Orban from the Press and Culture Department was. I met him for the first time when West Germany's Chancellor Helmut Schmidt visited Bucharest and extended credit guarantees of about $360 million in return for Ceausescu's pledges to facilitate the reunification of ethnic German families. He claimed that he worked for the Foreign Ministry, but I had no idea he was actually a Securitate colonel employed by *Serviciul "D"*— Disinformation. He looked like a decent, affable person, joined in pleasant and relaxed conversation, and he spoke German fluently. His mission was to discredit me in the eyes of my AP colleagues and damage my character. There were certainly interesting things between the dusty blue-and-cream covers of my Securitate dossier. I was a bit astonished, but I recovered quickly.

I came across several of his written reports, and there was one titled "OLT-81" in which he asked me and "Voicu" from ANSA (Gian Marco Venier, the correspondent of the Italian news agency) if we could write a story about the incidents in several cities in southern Romania where people had protested against food shortages. He wanted us to deny that these protests had a political connotation. We were aware of the unconfirmed reports. According to the reports, coal miners in Motru, Gorj County, protested against the lack of food and—most of all—the rationing of bread, a daily staple, to four hundred grams (fourteen ounces) a day per person. They were shouting, "We want bread" and "Down with Ceausescu." The government quickly met their requests, but not before the intervention of the army and the police, which forcefully stifled the revolt. More than a dozen miners were arrested, according to these reports.

I asked him why they didn't officially deny the reports, and Orban answered, "Because we don't have a Foreign Ministry spokesman." It was a cock-and-bull story from *Serviciul "D"*—of whose existence I wasn't aware at that time. Neither Venier nor I took him seriously. Let Agerpres or *Scanteia*, the Communist Party organ, write a story on this topic. Why was the Securitate getting into press matters? Not to inform but to misinform.

"There were some acts of hooliganism of some elements in some coal mining areas…elements who were shunning work, common infractors, against whom, naturally, the organs of order [i.e., police] took drastic measures," Orban wrote in his report that was annexed to my dossier. This was the same BS he told Venier who was known under the code name "Voicu" in their files.

"Yeah, sure, "some acts of hooliganism of some elements that were shunning work." Give me a break, comrade Orban," I told myself in the reading room of the National Council for the Study of the Securitate Archives. I remembered our conversation that took place in 1981.

I also recalled another meeting with diplomat-disinformer Moise Orban three years later when he came to the AP office to ask if I could write a story denying rumors of an alleged plot by the Romanian military to overthrow Ceausescu. I was aware of the rumors. According to them, their plan had failed, and several high-ranking officers—including two generals—were loaded in a helicopter and dropped in the middle of the Black Sea as punishment and fish fodder.

I could hardly stop myself from laughing. How could I write a denial of those unconfirmed reports without specifying an official source? A denial of such a delicate subject could not legitimately come from an anonymous source. That was the government's business. Why couldn't Agerpres write about this? Because the authorities preferred to keep mum rather than to risk opening Pandora's Box. Let *Serviciul "D"*—*Dezinformare* handle it; maybe they could do something. The rumors, though exaggerated, had a basis of veracity: several pro-Moscow army generals had planned a military coup, but the Securitate found out, and the generals were retired overnight. Working under Kremlin's protection, they were neither killed nor imprisoned.

Col. Orban left the office unhappy (but without threatening me), and it was the last time that we saw each other. I don't know if he had tried the same tactic with other foreign correspondents, such as Venier from ANSA or Markovic, from Tanjug (the Yugoslav press agency).

Eventually, the voluble "disinformer" Orban would get into trouble with his superiors, "being accused, despite repeated warnings, of frequently violating the labor norms in his relations with foreign citizens and the information-gathering network," as the Council would reveal later in a story posted on the internet. In a less verbose way, Venier told me before I left Romania that Col. Orban had been forced into retirement for being a womanizer and a drunk. His "disinformation" activity must have consumed him bit by bit, and he needed a refuge!

Hiding wiretaps in walls and under the floor to eavesdrop on people's conversations, tapping phones, opening letters, and monitoring the telex traffic of all foreign embassies and agencies were the faithful weapons of the regime for keeping the "golden dream" of the working class alive and vibrant.

On further leafing through my dossier, I found this note:

*UM0625*
*Nov. 17, 1979*

*To Special Unit "T"*

*As part of "THE FUTURE" plan of action, please start the monitoring of telex 11681 that belongs to the "Associated Press" press bureau in Bucharest, located at 30 Corbeni Street, 2nd floor, Apt. 4, instead of the telex post belonging to India's embassy in Bucharest.*

I was astonished! They were abandoning the Indians and monitoring the Americans? Couldn't they do both things at the same time? They didn't have enough technical capabilities? The budget allocated was too small? Baloney. There were no technical or financial limits when they really wanted to know something.

One day I got a telex from Larry Heinzerling, who was the director of AP's Central and East European Bureau based in Frankfurt. Incorporating the German Service of the AP, it was the agency's biggest news hub in Europe and the most profitable. He informed me that AP's president and general manager, Keith Fuller, would visit Romania as part of a whirlwind tour through the Soviet bloc that also included stops in Poland and Hungary. Accompanying Fuller was Richard O'Regan—who led the agency's news, photo, and business operations in Europe through much of the Cold War—and several US publishers of major newspapers, members of the AP news cooperative.

Romania's secret police used their entire arsenal of surveillance devices to find out what was discussed during the visit. To quote from my dossier, "The Securitate organs will take measures to ensure a complex and complete control over the activity the members of the delegation would unfold while they'll be in Romania."

I wasn't surprised about the details of the discussions that took place at the Foreign Ministry—where they met with Corneliu Bogdan, Romania's former ambassador to Washington—or at Agerpres—where the general director received them. They were the regime's trusted servants. But how did they learn about the contents of discussions during the dinner at InterContinental Hotel, where I was the only Romanian present? The "organs" did not ask me details, and even if they had asked me, I would not have told them. Or how did they monitor the conversations at a luncheon given by the US ambassador Rudolph Aggrey, who was known to the Securitate by the code name "Aron"? (I did not attend it.)

The Securitate must have used all the technical means it had in its arsenal both at the restaurant and in their rooms: wiretaps in ashtrays and flower vases (they were all over the grand table), double-bottom plates, and other special eavesdropping devices such as ACH, ACT, ATS, ICT, IDEB and who knows what else. I am also willing to bet my best pair of pants that the hotel's Gypsy band also "played" a part. The fiddlers, playing love songs ripe with the heartbreaking blend of anxiety, joy, love, surrender, and resolution, were carefully watching the Americans, who were enjoying the evening. They were trying to eavesdrop on the Americans' conversations by coming so close to the table that they almost touched the guests with their violins and bows.

In the car the next day, on our way to Agerpres, I explained to Fuller and the others a notable progression in the country's evolution. Before the war, Romania was renowned for the sophistication and refinement of its cuisine: French and Italian food for the rich, Greek and Turkish for the middle class, and Romanian *mamaliga* (polenta) for the poor. After the communist take-over, skill in meal presentation was replaced by the creativity in the hiding of microphones in ashtrays and flower pots and vases on restaurant tables.

Thumbing through my file, I came across a written report—several pages long—in feminine, tidy, calligraphic handwriting—of everything that had come under discussion at the dinner, Foreign Ministry, Agerpres, and the luncheon with the US ambassador. That is what "complex and complete control" is.

This detail is enlightening: "A source of our organs will offer herself to lead [the guests] on a visit to the Village Museum." I am not sure that such a visit took place, but they were meticulous to the smallest detail. After all, the "organs" did their duty for their Party and Homeland. I don't think that any other foreign trip taken by AP's top executives closely resembled their Romanian visit: wined, dined, and spied upon.

Being aware of the existence of "bugs," I was more guarded in my political comments at the InterContinental dinner party, but this worked to my advantage.

In a file memo after the visit, which I read in Vienna after I left Romania, Fuller would note the following:

Vio Urma is the most impressive prospect we met on our eastern European tour. He is bright, educated, and attractive. One of the first things that we noted favorably about him was that he felt no necessity of trying to impress us with how anti-Communist he is.

By frank responses to questions, he revealed a subtle understanding of the world he lives in [...] Urma has the potential to be a fine foreign correspondent if only one day we can get him out of Romania with his family.

That was very nice. Thank you AP President and General Manager Keith Fuller.

\* \* \*

If someone ever tried to get an idea of how many "bugs" Romania's Securitate had at its disposal, the number would probably match New York City's rat population. I am not talking about office and phone bugs. I found wiretaps at my parents' home where I lived. "Special measures were taken at the objective's domicile." That's how they put it nicely, as I saw in another note in my dossier. What "special" measures were taken exactly? (I found it interesting that instead of calling me by name, they used the neutral and politically correct "objective." They were "organs," and dubious individuals like me were "objectives.")

During the earthquake in 1977, when over one thousand people were killed in Bucharest, our two-story house (built in the 1920s) was severely damaged and required major repair work to its walls and ceilings, while a new tin roof had to be put in place of the old tiled roof. Years later, after another two earthquakes of lesser magnitude that necessitated other repairs, I found wires and what looked like eavesdropping devices buried in several walls—including the room where the AP telex machine had been installed temporarily.

\* \* \*

It seemed that the AP was not the only news agency interested in having a local reporter in Bucharest. After the Foreign Ministry had approved their request for a press office, the chief of the Reuters bureau in Vienna,

Sydney Weiland, was looking for an independent Romanian to do what I was doing.

I found a handwritten note in my dossier that was signed "Armasu." The person with this code name, a woman, was reporting that she had met with Weiland. The problem was that she was working for Agerpres, and Weiland didn't like it because he wanted to hire somebody with journalism experience but unattached to a state-run news medium. "Armasu" was unhappy too because, while Weiland didn't like the idea to hire such a person, Agerpres wasn't pleased either, as management had told her that since she was a Communist Party member, "I wouldn't be able to do what Viorel Urma does for the Associated Press." She wrote that "Agerpres's management described [Urma] as being a reactionary who does everything for money, without thinking of the consequences. When he [Urma] will stop being a correspondent, his future won't be too rosy."

Due to the "Armasu" source, I saw how the Agerpres executives labeled me: a "reactionary." And I had already read that the Securitate called me a "traitor" who "unfolds a hostile activity" by writing about "Romania's realities in a disparaging and defaming way."

The accusation that I was doing "everything for money" was by no means accurate. Weiland, whom I met for the first time at the press center during President Ford's visit, asked me bluntly if I wanted to work for Reuters, implying that they would pay me better. I told him that working for AP was more satisfactory for me.

Weiland's problem was that, after giving me permission to work for AP in Bucharest, the authorities would not allow other Romanians to be hired by the Western media. And foreigners wouldn't view the reporters that Agerpres would be willing to "lend" them in a positive light, as they were considered mere instruments of the Romanian government.

After the Foreign Ministry banned me from writing for AP, they told my superiors in Vienna and Frankfurt that they could ask for a Romanian replacement, and Agerpres would be ready to present them with "two or three" candidates from which to choose. But those "two or three" candidates would be the authorities' reliable hands, and they would work with Securitate approval, unlike me.

The Western news bureaus weren't going to fall for such a proposal.

\* \* \*

Tennis stylists have been trying for years to eliminate the word "love" from the game and vocabulary. Some umpires shout the words "nothing" or "zero" to make the score sound more competitive than social.

In what was described as the biggest love match on the courts since the Jimmy Connors-Chris Evert engagement in 1974 – which eventually ended in a breakup – Swedish star Bjorn Borg and his Romanian fiancee Mariana Simionescu wanted to restore the word "love" to tennis in all its cliché splendor.

Love match. Love story. Love conquers all.

Printed invitations began to circulate in Bucharest in the summer of 1980 for the wedding of the five-time Wimbledon tennis champion and his long-time Romanian girlfriend. And Romania's communist information apparatus was girding itself against a capitalist-style media event. The invitations, on glossy cardboard with inscribed golden letters, had been distributed by the bride's family. Printed at a state-owned publishing house, they misspelled the Swedish groom's name, calling him Born Borg.

According to initial reports, the wedding was to follow Romanian Orthodox Church ritual and be held at an island monastery in the middle of the Snagov Lake, the burial place of ruler Vlad the Impaler, better known in the West as Dracula. But Simionescu's family, fearing that "Dracula's" grave near the altar, where his decapitated body was laid, would not augur well for the couple's happiness, opted at the last moment for Caldarusani, a seventeenth-century monk monastery on a peninsula at another lake near Bucharest.

The site, although perhaps less picturesque, offered larger premises and did not oblige the wedding guests to carry garlic and crosses to repel the vampire. The couple and the wedding party was to feast at a plush Snagov villa rented from the Securitate for the occasion.

Snagov, Bucharest's best summer escape, was a village bordering the scenic lake with the same name. It was home to many international rowing regattas, and Romanian top officials, including Ceausescu, had summer retreats around the lake and an old forest.

The state-run media, eager to avoid the more sensational aspects of the event, clamped a blackout on the issue. Government officials were literally taken aback by word that more than one hundred foreign reporters, photographers and TV crew members planned to come and see the wedding, the most sensational bridal gathering in the post-war country.

From the Borg entourage, word spread that the hosts had asked Romanian officials to keep the press out of the wedding to which some coverage rights had been sold for large amounts of money.

I called Florea Tuiu at Agerpres to find out what kind of accreditation was necessary, if any, to cover the event. He expressed real worry that an invading army of news people would need "adequate facilities."

"It's a big problem," said Tuiu, who headed the agency's department reponsible for handling foreign reporters.

"You need a press center, telephones, telexes, operators, buses... Who will organize all this? We handle communist party congresses, conferences, state visits ... but weddings?"

Neither Borg nor his fiancee disclosed when permission was granted and by who. According to the constitution, Romanians could marry foreigners only if they got approval from the country's president or from the State Council.

Borg and Simionescu first met in 1974 but their romance exploded in the open during the French Open in Paris two years later. Things were not always so smoothly.

After the French Open, the auburn, hazel-eyed Simionescu had asked for politicl asylum in the United States, joining Martina Navratilova of Czechsolovakia as tennis defectors from behind the Iron Curtain. But she changed her mind after authorities blessed her marriage plans unexpectedly and permitted her to travel freely as her compatriot Ilie Nastase did.

Ceausescu was widely believed to have personally approved the love match. Also an important part in the scheme was apparently played by Mariana's father, an undercover Securitate colonel posing as a construction engineer with Arcom, a state building firm working overseas, according to Romanian sports writers.

As the day neared, the wedding route blossomed with police and potted palms for the first brief venture into the world's social spotlight.

"I'm a bit nervous" said mayor Dima of Bucharest's First District, one of several officials in line to marry the millionaire Swede and Simionescu.

"Weddings are pleasant for us but we have enough administrative problems to keep us busy," he said, as another wave of Swedish journalists marched past guards and up the hall being specially refurbished for the civil ceremony,

A platform covered in gold velvet was installed at the head of the hall, and gold and brown rugs laid for the guests. Officials pointed out where the couple would stand for the first of the two wedding ceremonies facing toward a huge Romanian official seal depicting mountains, sun, sheaves of wheat, and an oil derrick.

"This isn't our only preoccupation," said Dima, as workers washed the hall's marble corridors, scrubbed its marble staircase, changed its carpet and unloaded a new truckload of potted plants.

The room itself, not normally used for Romania's civil weddings, had been freshly painted a pale brownish pink and workers were still wiring it for camera lights and sound.

Borg and his fiancee, once a tennis player ranked 36th on the list of world's top female players, had remained secluded in the rented Securitate villa on the lakeside of the village of Snagov. Their privacy behind a sliding red, white and green gate was assured by police who said entry was by special permits only.

Another official and an army corporal were on duty at the isolated Caldarusani monastery, where the two were to have their second wedding of the day, one following the pageantry of the Romanian Orthodox Church.

When I went there one day before the planned wedding, the body of a local priest, ready for burial later in the day, lay in a coffin in a quiet corner of the three-domed church whose ochre and gilt interior was lavishly decorated with paintings of saints.

An official at the church warned that no photographs of the interior could be taken without permission from the Council of Socialist Culture and Education.

One of the monks living in the walled monastery, once a major cultural center before its communist reduction over years to a chicken and cattle farm, said the bride's family had requested as brief a ceremony as possible.

Several hundred people were expected to attend the weddings, as well as a reception afterwards at the Snagov villa.

A horde of foreign journalists, mostly Scandinavian, where to be kept outside both ceremonies and the reception. Borg's agents were reported to have sold exclusive coverage rights to some for healthy totals.

The Borg wedding, to be followed eventually by yet another party in Monte Carlo and a honeymoon in Spain, were part of a carefully arranged package whose costs remained a mystery.

People living in the rolling countryside around Caldarusani, a land of dirt roads, village wells, gypsy horse carts and tiled roof cottages, had heard a rumor that the Romanian arrangement alone cost Borg $1 million.

Simionescu earned respect around the place for her marital choice.

"She's a smart Romanian," said one villager, who seemed generally satisfied with both partners.

Steve Miller, who came from the Frankfurt bureau to cover the event, and I picked up the slightly drunk villager in our office car to show us the villa where the two were already consuming some of the "honey" in quiet surroundings, not far from the place where Ceausescu had his own palatial mansion.

"They have money, they are nice," he said. "Let God give them health. I just have money for cigarettes and *tsuica*."

When we arrived at the the well-guarded villa, a plainclothesman spotted the poorly dressed villager with his worn out hat on his head sitting in the front seat of the black-plated car, showing that it was owned by a foreign firm. (Cars owned by private Romanians carried white plates).

The man ordered him to get off and he faced a barrage of questions such as why was he riding in a foreign-owned car and what was his name. Contacts with foreigners, even when at stake was a wedding between two tennis players, were frowned upon by the guarding angels of Marxism-Leninism.

I got off the car to tell the official that I was a Romanian as well. An absurd and comic, almost Kafkaesque, dialogue ensued.

" Let him go, please. I took him to show us the way," I told the Securitate official.

"I didn't do anything wrong," said the villager, and a shade of concern passed on his wrinkled face.

"Why did you get into a foreign car?" the plainclothesman asked him.

"How could I know it's foreign?," the villager asked in his turn.

"It's not a foreign car. We bought it in this country and as you can see it's formally registered with the Romanian police. It's not a foreign diplomats' car, it has no CD plates," I said.

"I didn't do anything wrong, I swear on the icon of Virgin Mary," said the poor man, now really scared by the unexpected turn of events. "I've got three children and a wife. Let me go," he said, trying to kiss the hand of the official.

"You can go," the cop said pointing to me. "But you stay here," he told the villager, who had taken out his hat and pressed it in his hands nervously.

"Please let him go. What did he do?," I asked. "I'm traveling with a foreign correspondent, what will he say about this comedy?"

"You mind your own business," the cop answered back.

We had to leave the poor man at the authorities' mercy. I hoped that nothing happened to him for showing us the way to the villa.

The wedding day came on a hot July day and a large crowd, held back by squads of gray-shirted police, cheered as the blue-blazered Borg and his bride kissed under an archway of flowers and tennis racquets outside the city hall.

Mayor Dima, wearing a dark suit and his ceremonial sash of Romanian red, yellow and blue, pronounced the couple man and wife after a standard ceremony in the large meeting hall specially outfitted for the first jet-set wedding in Romanian history.

Fifty children in tennis shorts lined the steps of the hall, lifting racquets in their right hands and red and white gladioli in their left to form an archway under which the newly married couple emerged from the building.

Many guests, including the Swedish Davis Cup team, tennis stars John McEnroe, Chris Evert-Lloyd, Vitas Gerulaitis and Ilie Nastase along with Borg's trainer Lennart Bergelin, applauded when the couple were pronounced married and signed in an official register.

The bride and the groom had arrived at the town hall behind a police escort in a gray Swedish automobile still muddy from its drive into Bucharest from their secluded lakeside villa. The same car returned to take them back to the countryside for the Orthodox service in the isolated monastery.

Police were caught unprepared for their first encounter with a jet-set celebrity crush, one involving western press photographers and villagers who came from miles around in the countryside. Reinforcements were called in to deal with the crowds.

After their scuffle to get Borg and his bride safely into the monastery courtyard for the closed service, police cleared several hundred Romanian onlookers back from the gate. One boy and two men were ordered out of a tree, and two women were told to quit trying to build a scaffold to scale the monastery wall.

"They are like animals," one plainclothesman muttered of the arrival crush, which left scratches on the side of Borg's car and battered the traditional Romanian wedding candles, so long they stuck out the windows of the arriving autos.

Borg and his twice-wed bride, wearing a $7,000 silk dress embroidered with rhinestones and pearls, the creation of Ted Tinling, emerged from the monastery church in a shower of rice and tumbling photographers, toppled from chairs and ladders by the newly arrived traffic police.

Disco queen Regine and other ranking guests were transported in vans rented for the occasion down a tree-lined road, out of the monastery grounds on a path cleared among spectators and the monastery's wandering chickens and turkeys.

"They are trampling all of us," Borg's sun-tanned mother said, settling into her car after the ceremony performed by six Orthodox priests and four deacons.

Sometimes smiling, sometimes looking worried about the crush around them, the two walked inside a phalanx of traffic policemen out of the courtyard and to a nearby vicarage for more song and relaxation.

Although prices could not be confirmed, a priest said he had heard that the wedding feast was to cost $1,000 a head.

The monks at Caldarusani used to joke that the millionaire Borg, getting married at their church, might repair the potholed road leading out to the main highway to Bucharest. But their expectations waned on the eve of the wedding. Tradition dictates that the family of a Romanian bride makes a cash donation to the church involved.

Along those lines, one monk confessed, there had been hints to the family of Borg's bride that help in maintainig their ancient church would be appreciated. But the monks were reminded, he said, that it was Borg who had the money.

The Simionescus, about to acquire a new connection to a man expected to earn five million dollars that year, remained a family of "modest means," he said they were told.

The path to the old monastery remained unasphalted, but neither the marriage of the two would be spared of bumpy roads, and eventually Borg and Simionescu would separate after only four years.

By the time he retired from the circuit in 1983 at the age of 27, he was estimated to have amassed $75 million in prizes and endorsements.

# Interlude

The communist government closed the old AP Bucharest bureau, run by Leonard Kirschen, in 1950—after the Romanian was tortured into a false confession and charged with spying for the United States and Britain—becoming the first-known AP correspondent ever imprisoned. He was sentenced to twenty-five years in jail, but he was freed after ten years after the AP and the US State Department pressed hard for his release. Kirschen[11] was allowed to leave Romania and became a commodities reporter for AP in London. His book about his cruel confinement at the height of the Cold War, *Prisoner of Red Justice*, was published in London in 1963. It is the first prison report about Romania's Gulag.

Here are a few excerpts from his book:

*Now I was continually shadowed. Jeeps, Oldsmobiles, and new Fords trailed my car through the streets and along the roads out of Bucharest. All sorts of people were reading newspapers in front of my house and looking up at my window on the second floor. Whenever I went to official receptions, empty circles formed around me, and people would think twice before speaking to me. I found myself being cut off from all my regular press contacts. People at Agerpres, the Romanian News Agency, were always extremely "busy," and*

---

11 Having very good sources in Romania, one of Kirschen's AP scoops was about the forced abdication of King Michael under the communists' pressure in December 1947. All the other media got the news out a quarter of an hour later.

*I had to rely more and more on the official news bulletins. I grew depressed and nervous, expecting to be arrested every evening. It was impossible to escape across the frontier as the satellite leaders had agreed to return all escapees to their respective countries.*

*The authorities, however, were still biding their time with me. They realized that they could force the arrested Romanian staff of the [western] information offices to provide any evidence they needed against me. But they wanted something spectacular, for [...] I was the most active foreign correspondent in Bucharest, and over 80 per cent of the news coming from Romania was carried by the Associated Press. They also bitterly resented my continued visits to foreign legations despite the terror which had been unleashed. They knew that such visits profited both me and the Western diplomats who were being severed from their Romanian contacts, one by one. It was certainly not daring on my part but the conclusion that if I stopped my daily rounds, they would become doubly suspicious of my movements...*

*In this last period before my arrest, the Russian correspondents went to great lengths in being nice and in trying to convince me of the correctness of a public recantation. They wanted me to state openly that I was now seeing the true light; that I had been spying for Anglo-American Imperialist Agencies; and that the Associated Press was a vast world organization for spying against the working class and wrecking their happiness...*

*I and Marcel Pohne, my old friend of the United Press, knew that it was only a matter of days. The British and American diplomats were themselves in a panic by now, and their more honest servants revealed that they had been recruited to spy, under threat. The Securitate was installing microphones by means of frequent "inspections" from the telephone company. At the Athénée Bar, crowded in the past with foreigners, diplomats, and newsmen, only Pohne, [Raymond] Audibert [of France Presse], and I continued to turn up, for we knew that it made little difference any more. Afternoons and evenings grew more and more oppressive. To quarrel with a neighbor or hall porter was sufficient to bring the Securitate along. It was difficult to know whether one's closest friends were not in fact informers. Too often*

*they were! Arrests continued unabated. Treason, political organization, sab-
otage, incitement, agitation, and counter-revolutionary propaganda, were
amongst the infinite excuses to increase the terror. I completely stopped going
out at night and sat reading anything I could lay hands on…*

*The bell rang again. I went down to the entrance door and shouted: "Who's
there?" The reply came promptly: "This is the Securitate. Open up!" I did
so, and half a dozen men in light raincoats rushed in. Their leader flashed
a torch into my eyes and shouted: "Where's Leonard Kirschen?"*
    *"It's me," I replied.*
    *"Get back to your flat and dress," he ordered…*

*In the hall the night porter stared with frightened eyes and open mouth
at the midnight party. I was hustled into a sleek Oldsmobile and wedged
in between two of their agents at the back whilst the other three sat in the
front. As the engine started, one of the men beside me produced a pair of
motorbike goggles, covered with tin sheet. He put them on my nose and
tied them at the back of my head…"[12]*

* * *

*I plodded on painfully with the autobiography for some hours. The sun was up. The
trees outside the prison were alive with chirping sparrows. The light in the cell had
been turned off, and through the bars over the door, filtered sunlight disclosed a
bed bug crawling on the wall. Brown stains on the immaculate whitewash marked
the deaths of many others through former inmates. I crushed it with a bit of paper
and a fresh bloodstain began spreading. A few inches away, I spotted another bug
crawling along, then another yet another. I became engrossed in the hunt. "What
are you doing there? Spring cleaning? Leave that job to the DDT. You get on and
think," said the Eye. I tried to look like somebody who thinks. Yes, there was a lot
of thinking to be done.*

---

12  Leonard Kirschen, *Prisoner of Red Justice* (London: Arthur Barker Ltd, 1963, 10–13).

*Soon I was taken for further cross-examination, and the questions started all over again. "What do you know about [Donald] Dunham [chief of USA Information]?" but this time was Voice No 3. At noon I was taken back to my cell for food. Immediately afterwards the cross-examination continued. That night Voice No 2 returned. I did not know what they were after, and I did not know what they knew. I did not know what my crimes were, and I was ready to manufacture them. I had been under more than fifty hours of continual pressure without sleep and even before that, had little, since entering the prison.*

*At about midnight, the door of the little interrogation room opened. Somebody came in and sat down near the Voice. "Well, comrade, how's it getting on?" he asked. "He won't talk, comrade inquirer-general," replied the Voice. "He's beating about the bush and trying to fool us." The newcomer lit a cigarette, "Well, comrade," he drawled— noisily puffing smoke into the air—"there are several stages in a cross-examination. There is in this case as in all the others, the first stage, when the criminal will try to hedge and see what we know about his crimes. This is quite natural. All criminals hate the idea of being punished for their misdeeds. We must be prepared for this stage and have patience. I call it the period of incubation, and when it's over the eggs will be hatched all right. What do you think, Mr. Kirschen? Will you help us hatch the eggs? I mean will you cooperate with us in establishing the truth, or shall we have to soften you up? I would regret this second alternative very much because we're civilized people and don't believe in the use of violence." I sat silent not knowing what to say.*

*"I will help you," he continued after a while. "I will read you some excerpts from the public statement made yesterday at the trial of the Samuelli sisters [from the American and the British Press Offices] and the other bandits." He began reading passages in which they had declared that I was engaged in actively spying for British and American legations; that I had informed them of Soviet troop movements in Romania; and that I had given them information from which to judge the morale of the population, especially the peasants. On finishing he said: "Now you know where you stand. Even if you deny all this, we've enough evidence on hand to shoot you. You don't want to be shot do you? You're only forty-one years old, Mr. Kirschen, the best age in a man's life. You have plenty of opportunities ahead if, and I say if, you cooperate with us in establishing the truth. Go back to your cell and think it over. We shall assist you in every way if you'll only be cooperative. Don't forget we have all the means at our disposal, and if we*

*must use them, with the greatest of reluctance, we shall use them. If you insist on
behaving like a bandit, then we'll treat you like a bandit. Good night."*

*He left the room, and I was again alone with Voice No 2. "I advise you to
get back to your cell and begin your confession. Here are about a hundred sheets
of foolscap paper. If these aren't enough, knock at the door and ask for more."
The buzzer rang. "He goes back to his cell and writes," were the instructions as
I was hustled along with the goggles over my eyes. Back in the cell, I decided to
write a confession on the lines of the statements made in court. That would save
me the trouble of inventing something. Feverishly, I began scrawling and had
hardly finished when I was called out again. The Voice looked at my effort and
said: "Well, that's better, but I'm not satisfied. There isn't enough detail in what
you write. More detail and don't hide anything from us. We know everything."*

*After seventy-two hours of this routine, I was given a few hours rest every
morning. The interrogation continued through each afternoon and night till about
five in the morning. I had to write and rewrite the same thing over and over again.
This was done to find contradictions, which were inevitable, as it was impossible to
remember what one had written under such pressure. After two weeks Voice No 1
returned: "You remember me don't you? We met a fortnight ago. You're going to
work with me now. So far you've been fooling around with us, but now we must
get down to business. When it's all over, you will have a rest, read books, smoke to
your heart's content, eat what you want, and even play chess with another inmate.
But until then you must work, and that means you must tell us everything. You
must empty your mind before me. Have I made myself clear?"*

*From that moment on, for four weeks, day and night, with only a few hours'
rest in the late night and early morning, the cross-examination was renewed. What
did they want from me? In their frenzied hunt for spies, the regime were convinced
that the activities of the British Council and the United States Information Service
were nothing but a cover for a widespread net of intelligence agents. The government
was certain that they were holding the key man to this vast western enterprise. The
public would clearly realize that imperialistic forces do not hesitate to use every means,
however innocent, when it comes to destroying the welfare of the workers. Romanian
sympathy for the West would be considerably weakened. Admission from a correspondent of the largest Western News Agency (AP) that he had been engaged in espionage
would certainly confound the machinations of the western diplomats.*

*The second period of cross-examination covered my newspaper activity before the war, my work in Turkey during the war, and my return to Romania after the war. I was closely questioned about every member of the military and diplomatic missions to Romania with whom I had dealings. Especially the British and Americans. I was asked who I thought were spies and who not. I replied without hesitation that all were spies because they were working in the interests of their countries. This sweeping statement angered my interrogator who was concerned with those actually doing qualified intelligence work. But to the best of my ability I could not help him. The inquiry tried to prove that my "criminal activity" had begun with my postwar return to Romania, which had been organized by certain intelligence services in Turkey to establish a western spy net. It remained undecided whether I was spying for the Americans or the British.*

*They wanted to find out all my British and American contacts in the country. Not only my contacts but the contacts of my contacts were sought. Not only business facts but bed facts as well concerned them. Every little bit of scandal was received with joy. Not a single path was left unexplored. I imagined the indexing and cross-indexing that was going on somewhere as the information was checked and counterchecked. By this patient means of inquiry, which must be extremely costly, the dragnet is thrown and slowly pulled in. Everything that it catches is carefully examined, considered, and weighed. Years of such patient labor has led to the identification, indexing, and photographing of tens of millions of individuals all over the world with the careful annotation of their breakfast habits, virtues, and vices.*

*After foreign contacts, the inquiry turned to home contacts. Where did you get your information from? Here I had a field day. I put down the name of every Communist I had known in the Central Committee and in every government office and newspaper office I had entered. I gave them literally dozens of names, and the truth is in fact that all my information was accurate because it had come straight from members of the [Communist] Party. Though not one of them has ever been arrested for imparting it to me...*[13]

\* \* \*

---

13 Ibidem, 25–30.

*After several days [...] the interrogator suddenly seemed to go berserk. He began to rave and gesticulate violently. One day at the end of May 1950, he rang the buzzer and shouted: "This bandit goes for a walk. If he has anything to say, bring him to me."*

*I was led along the corridor with my goggles on and out into a courtyard. Then down a flight of stairs. With my goggles off, I found myself in a small cellar. In one corner a tiny cell had been partitioned off, complete with door and spy hole. Near the cell stood a small table with paper on it and a chair.*

*"Take your slippers off, they belong to the Republic, and you're now going to take a long walk. It wouldn't do at all to wear out the people's property with your walk." I took the slippers off and stood in my only pair of thin, badly holed stockings on the rough cement floor. "Get in," he ordered, pointing to the small cell. "Now just walk around the cell and think. You can go both ways if that's any help to you. But don't stop because you have to reach Brasov*[14] *as soon as you can.*

*"The quicker you get there the better, and don't forget to think. Get on with it!" I went in and began to walk around my cell.*

*The warder sat down at the table, opened a book, and began to read.*

*The door was open. From time to time he looked up, dissatisfied with the progress I was making, and shouted: "Come on! Quicker, quicker."*

*I walked around the cell, six feet by nine feet, for four days and four nights. Every six hours I was told to halt, and they threw in a dirty straw mattress covered with urine and bloodstains from the previous walkers. A straw pillow followed. I was allowed two hours' rest, and then the "manege," as it was called, began again. Round and round and round until my head spun like a top. When the six hours were up, I fell like a log on the mattress and went off into a heavy sleep. When I woke up and started walking again, my feet were swollen and aching as though on hot embers and sharp nails combined. At regular hours food was brought in, and I had to eat it standing, shaking violently and with bitter tears running down my face. Then I went off again on the endless trek. My warders changed every eight hours. Then I saw as in a dream that the warder was scribbling something on his paper.*

*I walked and cried. Death seemed a great relief but so difficult to find. I bumped my head against the wooden wall, longing for it. The warder lashed out at*

---

14 Brasov in Transylvania is one hundred and five miles from Bucharest.

*my feet with a belt. "Get moving. What d'you think you're doing?" he shouted as he tried to drag my feet along. If only the interrogator would call me I would admit anything. At the beginning of the third day, I was taken up to him. I was very weak and had lost a lot of weight. My colitis was acute. I went to the lavatory every hour and felt that all the water was running out of my body. He asked me: "Have you come to your senses?" I replied that I would sign anything he put before me. "You swine," he shouted "we don't want that. You want you to tell us what you're hiding from us. We don't want inventions. We want facts." The buzzer rang: "He continues to walk," was the order.*

*Back I was to walk again round the small wooden cell. The food remained untouched. My head was bursting; my bowels were one huge, empty sore. My raw stumps of feet were almost one with the molten quicksand on the floor. On and on through a nightmare space that surged and whirled, and sunk and soared. On and on in mindless chaos. After another day of it, I was led out goggled, through the courtyard and could feel the warmth of the May sun. Birdsong reached me faintly from the nearby acacias, amidst this gentle, surrounding peace. How incredible that hell was so near.*

*I had told them everything I knew, but it was all familiar to them. I realized with growing horror that if I did not produce anything fresh it would go on until they killed me. I made up all sorts of weird stories, each more fantastic than the other. Finally I managed to concoct something like a "reasonable" plot. I said that I had discussed with western diplomats the possibility of causing a rift in the Central Committee. I invented details of how we intended to buy influential members of the Central Committee. They then asked if I had actually approached anybody in this sense. I declared that their vigilance had prevented me. But with their suspicions aroused they wanted names of Party Members implicated, and I could not produce any. They questioned unexpectedly; had I known that Ana Pauker and other Communist leaders, then very much in power, had bank accounts in Switzerland? It appears that a Swiss newspaper had printed this story, and they assumed that I was connected with the source of the news. I realized that I had blundered and could not retreat because they were now convinced that the scent was hot. After three days of close questioning, they gave it up, but my confession took three pages in the court indictment. In fact my "invention" had become a main part of the indictment and proved far more harmful to me than all my previous, truthful statements.*

*Suddenly the inquiry ceased. At the beginning of June, I was placed in another cell with somebody else. Ten days later I saw the face of my interrogator for the first time. It was thin and intellectual. Balding and sallow, it had a familiar opaqueness and distance. He wore expensive, well-cut clothes and a massive gold watch. He told me that it was all over for the moment and that I could have books to read. He asked me if I wanted to be seen by a doctor and whether I had enough food. I wanted nothing and was grateful for the books. I felt as if I had come out of hospital after a critical illness, weak and shaky. Even with the lights on and the Voice materialized, I was afraid.*

*He explained: "Don't think the court is going to try you and decide on your fate. The dossier goes to them with our decision. We're the ones who'll decide on your punishment. The trial is just a formality. If you retract in court what you've told us here, we'll bring you back and take the hide off you. We've been very lenient and understanding in your case. We feel that you've been led astray by bourgeois influence and by the surroundings in which you moved. An intellectual has no business to be against the working class."*

*At the end of June I was called in daylight and asked whether I was satisfied with my food and whether I was receiving my cigarettes. But my interrogator's real purpose was to gloat. I heard from him about the Korean War for the first time and that in a few hours the Americans would be swept into the sea. "That's what's happening to the friends you think will come and save you. They need saving themselves. Yes, the Americans may have all the money in the world, all the arms and equipment, but they lack the spiritual arms and ideals. They don't know what they're fighting for. We Communists know what we want, and we're going to get it. We have the men and the ideals," he concluded.*[15]

---

15 Ibidem, 30–33.

## 7

*To General Iulian Vlad*
*Comrade minister,*

*I bring to your attention the annexed materials with the*
*explanation that Viorel Urma, a Romanian citizen, is the*
*author of other materials, which cause harm to our country…*

—ADRIAN IONESCU, DEPUTY GENERAL DIRECTOR OF
AGERPRES

Bucharest
1984

1984 was Orwellian for me. It seemed to reflect George Orwell's satirical novel about an ideal (utopian) society where the government is almighty and dictates the people's everyday lives. Ceausescu's Romania was the perfect image of such a world. And the Big Brother, the Securitate, was watching so that nobody dared to move a finger. At least that's what they wanted people to believe.

My fate was sealed that year.

Leafing through my Securitate dossier, I came across the note written by Adrian Ionescu to General Iulian Vlad, deputy interior minister and future head of the State Security Department. What did I do to provoke the former Agerpres correspondent to Vietnam—he himself a Securitate general under cover, according to some? I quote from his letter, which I found in my dossier: "Urma's stories on the government decree about the registration of the means of printing and their use, as well as (the stories) about the so-called crime phenomena and some 'problems' in our society have led to the launching of hostile acts by some circles in the Western media."

Western media outlets were writing the truth about what was happening in the country, and the truth was considered a "hostile act." Nineteen eighty-four reincarnated! Romania upside-down.

The story about the typewriter owners who were required to provide type sample of numbers and letters for registration with the police, was interpreted as a "hostile act." According to the law, typewriters were to be denied to people who had a criminal record or posed a "danger" to public order or state security. Penalty for failure to comply with the law was $240 and the confiscation of the offenders' typewriters. In addition, ordinary Romanians were banned from owning or using copiers. Romania was the only Soviet-bloc country that had passed such a law, designed to curb clandestine leaflets that were critical of the regime.

I had an animated debate on this topic with Florea Tuiu, Agerpres's former correspondent to Japan, who often met with visiting or Bucharest-based foreign reporters. He invited me to his office, wanting to know why I wrote that story.

"Why not?" I answered. "It's not a state secret."

"The decree was published in the *Official Bulletin*," I continued. The *Bulletin* published all the bills, presidential decrees, government ordinances, and other major legal acts.

"Fine, but it wasn't published by newspapers; the *Bulletin* is not a press organ," he said.

"Is it official?" I said. "It is." I answered my own question.

"It was a wrong decision by you. You should be more careful," he said, looking obliquely at me in disapproval.

In their minds, this law was only for domestic consumption. Writing about it in the foreign media was considered a crime. That's why the regime buried it in the *Official Bulletin*, which they considered outside the interest of Western reporters. Luckily, we had a subscription to the publication and received it by mail. The story was a big scoop for AP.

I found a long written note in my dossier at page 118 about Ionescu's complaint. I have no idea who "Cornel," its author, is. Here is the gist, verbatim:

*"CORNEL"*                                 *STRICT SECRET*
*Casa: "UNIC"*                           *Exemplar unic*

*Nr. 001712/18.1.1984*

*NOTE*

========

*For a story by "ASSOCIATED PRESS" Agency, referring to what he called "the campaign in Romania against crime and corruption," VIOREL URMA, the correspondent of this agency to Bucharest, was summoned to the Press Center at Agerpres for explanations because he falsely presented certain deplorable acts committed by some individuals who violated the law…*

*"The publication of some data on crimes and the punishments applied seem to reflect a concern of [the country's] leadership for the observance of law and the maintenance of order. Various publications have started recently to publish weekly columns dealing with such infractions in a clear effort to discourage those who would intend to commit them…" [the note quoted from one of the stories I wrote].*

"CORNEL" went on with his own comments: *Apparently, these are (Romanian) pickup stories but presenting them in "medallion" and neglecting other important problems that a country faces, such materials display a hateful and one-sided picture of Romania.*

*These [AP] stories were recently broadcast by "RADIO FREE EUROPE" which evidently blames the regime, the "precarious social and living conditions," the "lack of civic education and the presence of corruption," the note said.*

*Therefore, in this context, URMA shows a particular interest for such stories. He was the first who wrote about the registration of typewriters with the police, transmitting through the American Agency "ASSOCIATED PRESS" the following: "The measure was taken to prevent the distribution of critical leaflets. Through this measure the regime tries to ban the [illegal] publication of written materials, produced by ethnic Hungarians, Germans, and other nationalities, who complained about the intensification of persecutions in recent months…"*

"CORNEL"

*OFFICER'S NOTE*
============

*The note was taken as part of the intelligence surveillance of [URMA] and would be used by Serviciul 1 [counterintelligence], which has him in their attention.*

*I suggest that we analyze the situation of this "ASSOCIATED PRESS" correspondent with Serviciul 1 to see to what extent he will be invited to press activities in the future…*

The Romanian media devoted growing attention to fighting corruption, and the campaign had intensified with the regime's approval. There were weekly stories of severe punishments meted out for those who were stealing from the "public wealth," reflecting the growing concern of authorities about economic crimes at a time when Romanians suffered from food and energy shortages, and economic stagnation in general.

Among the most serious corruption cases were three men who were sentenced to death for stealing meat from a processing plant in southern Romania and selling it for profit to local restaurants and food stores. The trio was charged with "undermining the national economy" and shot. How could two hundred pounds of meat "undermine" the country's Marxist economy?

Other press stories castigated what they called "cemetery hyenas" who stole flowers from graves for resale and wooden crosses to burn in winter for heating. At other times, offenders in Bucharest and other cities "robbed" street sewage canals of their lids to sell them as scrap iron.

In their "blame game," the authorities were trying to put the onus for the deepening of the country's economic crisis not on Ceausescu's failed industrialization policies but on "déclassé individuals" and what they called "harpagons, rats and sharks." Romania was a free country "with some problems," they said, but its people were leading a good life. The food and other shortages were due to "greedy and rotten elements," such as administrators and stores managers, who were "sabotaging economic activities" in order to enrich themselves.

These "pickup stories presented in medallion," namely the grouping of several official stories on the same subject in a bigger story with the required political background and context, disturbed the regime to such a degree that they summoned me for "explanations" and intimidation. But where was I misrepresenting the facts? Was I fabricating them? The facts were official information…but the conclusions were not!

That's how you could creatively use the information published in the state-controlled media. It's like making Chicken Francaise with spaghetti (the Romanian non comestible recipe): You start with official info, such as the typewriters' decree, you mix it with details from other cookbook recipes (stories in the daily *Scanteia*, or other state-run media), you add unofficial ingredients from your sources (my father's story who had to go the police in person to register his typewriter although he was eighty years old), you add salt and pepper…and the dish is ready to be served (published). Some will like it (Western media), others will find it indigestible (authorities)…and the chef (the writer) will get screwed, but those are the risks of the job.

I found several of my own stories in my dossier that were given as examples of my "hateful and one-sided picture of Romania."

Among them was a 750-word story about the huge scandal with international overtones between the chief rabbi Moses Rosen and the nationalist poet Corneliu Vadim Tudor. Another was about Ceausescu's anti-corruption campaign and the real meanings of it. Both were translated into Romanian by Agerpres for "internal use," that is for the information of Party officials in charge of press censorship and the Securitate.

In the incident that caused international reverberations and involved Romania's Jewish community, Rosen had accused a "gang of neofascists and hooligans of the pen" of spreading the "anti-Semitic poison" in a book of poetry written by Tudor, one of Ceausescu's court poets and flatterers.

The book, *Saturnalii*, was banned two months after its publication, but the state-controlled media kept silent on the scandal. Not a single word was published on the topic in the country.

Rosen, who in fifty years as chief rabbi oversaw an exodus of nearly 400,000 Romanian Jews to Israel, told me in an interview that the book contained many anti-Semitic references and some direct attacks against his person, such as these lines: "Sad gambler, you, monument of hatred/Satyr draped in purple shroud" (purple was the color of his official cloak). The poem also contained expressions such as "traitor without a homeland," "offender," and "you'd better sell buttons and raki" (a reference to the Jewish grocery shop owners before the war). Even worse, Moses Rosen said, there were combinations of words that referred to him by his name: "Small ecchymoses [sic] are your eyes of beast" and "You sat on roses [sic] in your warm den."

Rosen sued Tudor[16] for "propaganda against socialist order," chauvinism, and "insults to state dignitaries." According to Romania's penal code, these accusations were punishable for up to fifteen years' imprisonment. (No trial ever took place.) He also said he requested a meeting with Ceausescu to complain against Tudor. According to Rosen, Jewish leaders such as Edgar Bronfman, president of World Jewish Congress, had written to Ceausescu to express their indignation. Romania was the only Soviet-bloc country that had diplomatic ties to the Jewish state, and Israeli leaders, such as prime ministers Menachem Begin and Shimon Peres, came to Romania at various times to discuss the Arab-Israeli conflict with Ceausescu, in which the Romanian leader pursued a mediating role.

---

16 After Ceausescu's overthrow, Tudor was the leader of the Greater Romania Party—which espoused strong nationalist and anti-Semitic views—and a member of the European Parliament. In 2004, Nobel Peace Prize laureate Elie Wiesel returned the *Steaua Romaniei* (The Order of the Star of Romania) medal, one of the country's highest honors, after President Ion Iliescu awarded Tudor the same distinction. Wiesel said he was returning the honor because he could not "accept being placed on the same level" as Tudor.

Another story that I found translated into Romanian was about a series of gun and bomb attacks involving Arab citizens in Romania. In the country, bomb explosions and gunshots were something as rare as a gourmet burger at your favorite restaurant.

A bomb that exploded while they were searching the car of a Syrian student had killed two members of a bomb-defusing squad. It was the most serious incident in a series of bomb threats involving Syrian and other Arabs in Bucharest. There were ten thousand Arab students in the country, and some of them attended special courses in guerrilla training.

The day before I wrote the story, a car parked in front of the building where the AP office was located was suspected of having a bomb in it, and the police had to evacuate all tenants. Among them were Arab diplomats, my next-door neighbors, and this is how I learned about what was happening. Outside the building, I watched how an army bomb-disposal unit searched a white Mercedes after they enclosed it under one-inch thick steel plates. According to the diplomats, the car belonged to a Syrian student who had received a phone call and a warning that a bomb would explode in his car. He said he called the Romanian police, who searched the car, but no bomb was found. Several months before, a man armed with a gun had shot and killed a Jordanian diplomat while he and his five-year-old son were getting out of a hotel in downtown Bucharest. The Palestinian group Black September later took responsibility for the attack. A Romanian police officer told me that the bomb attacks seemed to be a result of accounts being settled between Arab groups in Romania and that no Romanian citizens were involved.

Supposedly compounding my guilt for writing these stories was the fact that Radio Free Europe had broadcast them for their Romanian listeners. Now everybody knew what I had been writing about!

A few years before, the military center of the 1st District where I lived had sent me a notification through a military courier for a four-week call-up as they badly needed English translators. I talked to the colonel in charge of the center, and I explained my situation to him. He said they were short of translators for English speaking "guests" and couldn't help it. Guests? It was an open secret that Romania was home to Arab and African commandos trained in guerrilla warfare as Ceausescu had cordial relations with PLO leader Yasser Arafat, Libyan strongman Moammar Gadhafi, and various African independence movements. There were training centers at Branesti and Posada, east and north of Bucharest, and in other parts of the country. As Romanian instructors did not speak English, and the "guests" didn't speak Romanian, they needed interpreters.

Due to the nature of my job, I did not consider myself to be a suitable candidate for this kind of activity. I didn't want to get involved in this and later on be formally charged with espionage. I had no idea if this was a deliberate setup to see how I could react (and if I took the bait) or if the military center was honestly unaware of what I was doing.

I thought that my interaction with the colonel had solved the problem, only to find out a day later that he had called home and talked to my mother while I was at the office. He warned her that if I didn't show up for the call-up, they would "put me in chains." I decided to make as big a fuss as possible. Therefore, I messaged my superiors in Germany about the threat, and I asked for a meeting with officials at the Ministry of Defense. The next day I went and talked to a general from the public information department who asked me for a written explanation of the reasons for which I refused to obey the call-up order. They accepted them, and that was the end of it. The next day the Securitate called me at the office asking if my problem had been resolved. After seeing my forceful reaction, they wanted to make sure that things wouldn't get out of control—especially after Sandy Higgins, the AP chief of bureau in Bonn (which was a key outpost near the European front of the Cold War) asked me in a telex message: "Are you OK? Did they put you in chains?" (I met Sandy after the devastating 1977 earthquake in Romania in which more than 1,200 people died, which we both covered.)

In my Securitate dossier, I found only four of my stories given as examples "to document my betrayal activity." "That wasn't very many articles," I told myself, thinking that other stories about Romania should have been even more offensive in the authorities' eyes. I had written about the miners' strikes in 1977; Romanians' unheated homes in the winter due to the energy crisis; the growing food shortages and the protests and jokes on this topic (the pig's hooves were derisively called "Adidas" and the pig's ears were "radars"); Ceausescu's program of "rational nutrition," which was meant to hide the food crisis; the education tax for Romanian emigration seekers; the taxes on ethnic Germans of up to 11,000 DM or on Jews of around $8,000 per person for being allowed to settle in Germany and Israel (in fact their "sale" for the payment of Romania's foreign debt); the tax for families without children of up to $35 dollars a month (derisively called "the dick tax"); the demolition of churches and old districts in Bucharest to make room for the *Conducator's* grandiose project *Casa Poporului* (People's House), a Babylonian-style construction and the second largest building in the world after the Pentagon.

But where was the alleged espionage activity they suspected me of? Perhaps they thought I was spying when I was traveling in our office car to the towns around Bucharest looking for food available only on the black market, such as meat and cheese.

I was aware that I was under their surveillance, and I was trying to take the best precautionary measures. I didn't meet face-to-face with Western diplomats, preferring to call them when I had questions. Our phones were tapped, so the "organs" were aware of the content of our discussions. I found many telephone notes in my dossier, actually surveillance records, about my conversations with US diplomats.

Here is an example:

*11.02/ 1980*

*"SANDA"*

*Time 1530 [3.30 p.m.]. Viorel Urma from Associated Press speaks to Perlman saying he was notified that a US delegation arrived in Bucharest to carry talks on human rights with Ministry of Foreign Affairs officials.*

SANDA was the Securitate's code name for the US Embassy, and Perlman was the American press attaché.

Here is another record:

## "SANDA"

*22.02.1980*                                                              *UM0625/311*

*Time 1226. Viorel Urma from Associated Press in Bucharest calls Perlman to say that the president and general manager of AP, Keith Fuller, will visit Romania in the spring and would like to meet with "ARON" on May 12, 1980.*

"Aron" was the code name for US Ambassador Rudolph Aggrey. *Unitatea Militara* 0625 belonged to the 3rd Directorate for Counterintelligence.

While I kept my contacts with Western diplomats to a minimum, I went rather often to the American Library to read newspapers, see movies, and borrow books. The Big Brother was watching:

## NOTE

*We'd like to let you know that Urma Sergiu from Bucharest, Campina Street 8, was invited by the American library in Bucharest to attend a conference with slides on July 12, 1983, and also on July 27 at 16 hours [4 p.m.]*

Secondly, I had to be prudent with those who came to our office to tell me about cases of human-rights violations and asking me to write about them.

Once I received a visit from a young man who took a bottle with a red liquid in it out of his pocket. He said the "organs" had beaten and kicked him in his kidneys and that he was urinating blood. How could I verify this? I had to be careful and use all my diplomacy and tact. How could I know he hadn't been sent by the Securitate to see my reaction? This type of thing happed to me more than once.

I came across an information note from "Horia" who had paid a visit to the office in March 1983. He came to tell me that a Romanian citizen with a valid passport had gone on a hunger strike because the Israeli embassy had turned down his petition for an entry visa. Would it be possible to write a story about this case—not only about Romanians who wanted to emigrate to the West and were refused a passport by the communist authorities? I told him that I didn't know who this person was and what his problems were. He was visibly angry at my answer. Years later, I would read a report from his visit in my dossier.

*Regarding Mr. Urma, he made me an impression of an uncooperative person, having a tendency to refuse. He is aware of this characteristic and of the fact that he is not suitable for his job, and he tries to attenuate his repulsive character through vague promises like "we'll see what we can do," "we'll talk about this later," etc.*

### "HORIA"

That was total hogwash!

Judging by the semiliterate style and the stupid things he wrote about me, he seemed like a person with a screw loose. If the Securitate made use of sources like "Horia," I had a good explanation for the idiocies that people found in their Securitate dossiers. These sources, "Horia, Cornel, Tudora, and Andrei" are mentioned several times in my file. I wish I knew who they were.

How do you write stories in a totalitarian system where censorship controls the channels of information? One needs to be creative and use all possible means and (re)sources.

I needed all my creativity when I wrote a story in the aftermath of Ion Mihai Pacepa's defection to the United States. Pacepa, a three-star Securitate general and one of the highest-ranking defectors from the Soviet bloc, had vanished in July 1978 while on an official trip to West Germany. A month later, I was invited—along with other foreign reporters—to the official stand for the August 23 military parade, Socialist Romania's

National Day. One row behind me, I heard several voices talking about seven Securitate generals who had been "swept away." They were saying that other purges were to be expected. They were talking aloud about a major reorganization of the department (of foreign intelligence) and that a large number of officers would be affected.

Rumors about major changes within the Securitate and the Ministry of Internal Affairs were circulating in the weeks that followed Pacepa's defection. According to these unconfirmed reports, scores of officers were under investigation at Securitate's Rahova penitentiary to determine if they had any connection with Pacepa's defection. Actually, the changes had begun in the spring when Army General Nicolae Militaru had been uncovered as an agent of the Soviet military foreign-intelligence service (known by its Russian GRU acronym).

I had no idea about the identity of those who were talking about the purges following Pacepa's flight. I didn't turn my head, but I pricked up my ears. They could be Foreign Ministry, Army, or Party Central Committee officials, who knows? They talked openly and loudly, without giving any names. Perhaps they were eager to vent their own frustrations. Maybe they were expressing their joy over so much "sweeping." But, clearly, they were talking about Pacepa. I needed a confirmation of those rumors, and I had it now, somehow. After I returned to the office, I wrote a short story, based on "informed sources" and the unconfirmed reports that were already circulating. I also mentioned that the official media in Romania weren't saying a word about the case.

After Pacepa's defection, which destroyed Romania's foreign-intelligence network, Ceausescu had a nervous breakdown and gave orders for his assassination. Pacepa, who was also Ceausescu's adviser for national security and technological development, received two death sentences, and the Romanian leader decreed a bounty of $2 million for his death.

During the 1980s, the Securitate enlisted Venezuelan terrorist Ilich Ramirez Sanchez known as "Carlos the Jackal" to assassinate Pacepa in America in exchange for one million dollars. Documents found in the Romanian intelligence archives show that the secret police had given

Carlos a whole arsenal to use in "Operation 363" for assassinating the general, including plastic explosive, submachine guns, and grenades.

Speaking about sources and resources, Romania was shaken in 1982 by a huge scandal involving the Transcendental Meditation (TM), a movement that had spread rapidly through its intellectual elite. In the end it was disbanded by the regime, and the followers were chastised. More than three hundred college professors, scientists, writers, and artists were expelled from the Communist Party and fired from their jobs—among them Andrei Plesu, Mihail Sora, and Marin Sorescu, who were big names in Romanian culture. For the regime, the TM was considered a "sect espousing neo-fascist ideas to undermine the socialist order and lead to anarchy and even counterrevolution." As a result of the scandal, the minister of education was dismissed, as well as the director of the Institute of Pedagogic and Psychological Research. The institute was shut down and dismantled, and yoga and other forms of spiritual and relaxation practice were banned in Romania—the only East European country to take such a harsh step. Who would have thought that the Hindu spiritual discipline, whose aim was to attain bodily and mental control and well-being, would pose such a great danger to communism? "Transcendental" sounded dubious, like a reactionary bourgeois enterprise (apart from the fact that Ceausescu and other Party luminaries couldn't even pronounce the word).[17]

The story I wrote on this topic was a scoop, using the information provided by my mother-in-law, a secretary in the Ministry of Education, and balancing it with the official position promoted in the monthly *Pentru Patrie* (For Homeland), issued by the Interior Ministry. According to the magazine, TM was a sect whose aim was "world domination," no more, no less.

Here is another example of creative use of the situation on the ground. It was not known if Romania would take part in the Los Angeles Summer Olympics after all the other Soviet-bloc countries had announced that they would boycott the event. The official media were mum. The sports officials I talked to claimed they didn't know anything. I had an idea: I

17 Twenty years later, Chinese officials reacted against the Falun Gong spiritual movement in a similar way as the Romanian authorities. Both movements were seen as a potential threat due to a perceived independence from state and their spiritual teachings.

could go and check all the big stadiums in Bucharest to see if any athletes were training for the games. At the Dynamo Stadium, a big padlock on the main-entrance gate welcomed me. That was unusual, so I scaled a brick wall. Nobody was inside. However, I saw a poster on which was written "We wish our athletes success at the Olympic Games." Aha! Glued on a large window were several lists of names and the sporting events each athlete was expected to participate in. I was ready to scale the wall again to get out when a security guard saw me and asked, "How did you get in here?"

"I'm an Associated Press reporter," I answered. "I'm looking for the president of the track-and-field association. I was told that he will be here this morning. Why don't you keep the gate open? I had to scale a wall to get in."

"Oh," the guard said deferentially. "You work for Agerpres. There's nobody here now; all of them are in a training camp near Bucharest."

I didn't correct him. If he thought I was an Agerpres reporter, so much the better. I said aloud, "I'm sorry to bother you. They gave the wrong information, and I wasted my time."

I asked him a couple of questions, and I gave him a 10-lei bill for a bottle of wine. Then I asked him to open the gate so I could leave with dignity and well informed. With what I knew already, I wrote a story about Romania's participation at the 1984 Summer Olympics, and I sent it to our bureau in Vienna. At the Los Angeles games, the Romanian athletes got the second spot in the medal totals, behind the United States but ahead of West Germany. Although I had an invitation from AP to cover the Romanian athletes, the authorities did not allow me to leave the country.

I was not surprised that they didn't let me go. At least the story was a scoop.

It wasn't always like this.

I remembered another sporting event, back in October 1972, when Catinca Ralea, my boss at Radio Bucharest, sent me to cover a Davis Cup encounter in which Romania played the United States. It was the first Silver Bowl final in an East European country.

"You do a daily reportage for our English-speaking listeners overseas, with description, interviews, analysis, comments ... everything. Good luck," she said.

Ceausescu saw sport as a way to safely build nationalism and prestige, and the entire city was in the grip of the unprecedented event. However, the atmosphere was quite panicky.

I went to the airport to interview captain Stan Smith and coach Dennis Ralston. Tension and security were so high, that when the Air France jet arrived at Otopeni about two dozen Romanian SWAT elite troops, carrying machine guns and having knives strapped to their ankles, greeted the Americans on the tarmac.

Five weeks earlier at the Munich Olympics, Arab terrorists had killed eleven members of the Israeli Olympic team. The terrorists, calling themselves Black September, threatened to cause turmoil in Bucharest, as the Americans had two Jewish players.

The guests were so concerned, both about the threats and about the partisan crowd of screaming Romanians, more accustomed to attend football (soccer) games than tennis, that Ceausescu felt obliged to assure Nixon, his friend, that "everything will be fair play, without incidents."

"Extraordinary security was set up around the American team and its two Jewish members, Harold Solomon and Brian Gottfried. Romanian President Ceausescu let it be known that heads would roll if there was a hint of an incident," wrote Curry Kirkpatrick for *Sports Illustrated*. "As a result, the US players walked, talked, rode in private limousines, took meals and practiced while surrounded by 20 unsmiling secret police, officially known as 'translators.'"

"The American team lived in isolation on the 17th floor of the sparkling new InterContinental Hotel," Kirkpatrick continued. "They were watched by monitored cameras. They rode a private elevator. They were not allowed near windows, and they disappeared nightly upstairs to eat meals with their guards and watch movies sent over by the US Embassy."

Smith and Tom Gorman represented the US in singles. Smith and Erik van Dillen teamed up in doubles. Lining for the Romanians: the volatile Ilie "Nasty" Nastase and the bearish Ion Tiriac.

In the end, the American players won the best of five series, 3-2.

It was a huge disappointment for the Romanian hosts. So what happened to my "daily reportage for our English-speaking listeners overseas"? (I doubt that there were more than one hundred such listeners in the whole world, mostly in Africa and India, interested in the station's pro-Ceausescu propaganda. Occasionally we received letters from them).

After the first two singles, the result was a tie, 1-1, so I was awarded ten minutes of broadcasting time to describe what happened. The next day, the Americans won the doubles and my time was cut down to three minutes. On the third day, Nastase leveled the series at 2-2 by beating Gorman and setting up a decisive match between Smith and Tiriac, which the composed American won.

"Forget everything you did. We'll mention only the result, without any details or comments. It would have been a different story had we won the final," Catinca said.

Journalistically speaking, the whole thing was a fiasco for me, although I prepared the best as I could. However, it wasn't my fault. At least I had the occasion to see a Davis Cup final, unlike my colleagues who watched it on TV.

Meanwhile, my relations with Romanian officials were deteriorating. I came across this piece of information:

*NOTE*

*May 17, 1984*

*In January 1984, Urma Sergiu Viorel was warned by the Agerpres management because he transmits almost exclusively stories that create for the American public opinion a distorted image about some aspects of the realities in our country. The measure [i.e., warning] was without result, (Urma) continuing to adopt a hostile attitude and publish articles with a disparaging character about RS Romania.*

I recalled what Captain Sandulescu had written in his log (which was attached to my dossier) after one of his visits to the office: "Since (Urma) is a person with which practically it's not possible to have a constructive dialogue, he's investigated by means of an individual surveillance dossier for the documentation of activity of treason and for his removal from his current job…"

Before getting out the door, he made this chilling comment: "Of all the Romanians which Ludington met with and befriended, you are the only one left in the country. All the others are gone. They evaporated."

Was it the last warning? Was it a suggestion that I'd better leave the country—or else? I recalled the Securitate's determination to go after Ludington's contacts. They kept track of everybody he had contacts with, and they knew what happened to them, whether they emigrated or stayed in Romania. Good grief!

After thirty years, I still have questions: How could they document my "treason" activity when I was not a traitor? What was I betraying? The lies about the *Conducator's* "Golden Epoch"?

It is unclear to me what they meant by "his removal from his current job." Physical removal? Car accident? Prison? Would we be going back to the 1950s when Kirschen was accused of trumped-up espionage charges and spent ten years in prison, being subjected to methods of bestial cruelty?

What kind of a country was Romania where two AP correspondents and Romanian citizens were labeled "spies" and "traitors"? Romania was truly a "maverick" country, but not for the reasons usually cited.

Things like these did not happen anywhere else in Eastern Europe. These were the characteristics of the Romanian communism: its harshness, the excesses of the repressive police machine, and the cowardice and servility of those who supported it. Add to that the personality cult—what the Romanians candidly call *pupatul in cur* (ass kissing)—that has long traditions in Romanian history and the general lack of honor that people developed as a result of routinely trying to adjust to hostile historical conditions by keeping their heads low in order to survive. Romanians are not like the Poles or the Czechs, and I, as a Romanian born individual, am saddened to admit this.

This is what Romania was all about—not its much-trumpeted independence from Moscow or its would-be opening to the West, as some thought until Pacepa's defection. The Securitate had no idea what he had concocted through the years and what his real plans were. A traitor or not, he fooled them as if they were a bunch of incompetent dunderheads—which indeed they were!

\* \* \*

Tudor, the orifice of jingoism and chauvinism, was one of the most devoted bootlickers of the presidential couple. Here is an example in his artistic style:

Season's Greetings
Greatest woman seen so far
Of the whole of our nation
She's the heavens brightest star
Clad in the Romanian fashion.
It's Elena Ceausescu
Purest is her vibrant aim
The best mum to our rescue
Coming with a science brain.
Her accomplishments are greater
Aiming high as our guide
In supporting our Leader
Standing proudly by his side.[18]

This poem was dedicated to Elena, Ceausescu's wife, who was number-two in the Communist Party hierarchy after her husband. Though an elementary school dropout, she obtained a PhD in polymer chemistry and was officially adulated as a "scientist of world repute."

18  Published in *Saptamana* weekly, January 6, 1984. English version by Constantin Roman, London, 2012.

## 8

*This to inform you that on August 3 the ONT Litoral tourism office will be visited by Rosenblum Mort-Lee, an American citizen and a special correspondent of Associated Press agency and Urma Viorel, a Romanian citizen. Please take measures for positively influencing Rosenblum Mort-Lee and for his complex control, including [the use of] special means [to monitor] his activity...*

—Telex message from the Department of State Security to the chief of Securitate of Constanta, a port city on the Black Sea (Note found in my Securitate dossier, July 1983)

Golden Crown Hotel, Bistrita
Summer 1983

I am traveling with Mort Rosenblum, one of the few AP special correspondents, to the Borgo Pass and the town of Bistrita in Transylvania, looking for Dracula.

I drive our office car, a Czech-made Skoda 120, which I affectionately (and cynically) nicknamed the "Swan of the Balkans." Nicolae Paduraru, a Tourism Ministry official and guide, accompanies us on our odyssey.

Rosenblum, who in his distinguished journalistic career covered coups, earthquakes, and major political events across the world, is a first-time visitor to Romania. He plans to write several stories, one of them on Count Dracula—who has entered the American subconscious like McDonald's hamburgers and french fries with ketchup. In Japan and the

West, including Canada, the bloodsucker's legend sells better than any of Ceausescu's "selected works" about Romania's forced industrialization. Let the psychoanalysts figure out why Dracula gets so much attention overseas, while at home most Romanians give the legend the cold shoulder.

Apart from the vampire, Rosenblum wants to do a story about Black Sea tourism in a time of food and gasoline scarcity (outweighed by an abundance of police presence) and rationed entertainment. The authorities had decreed that restaurants and nightclubs must shut down by midnight at the latest to allow tourists to get a good night's sleep. In beds, people usually do other things than debating how to overthrow the government.

Years in the future, thumbing through my Securitate dossier, I came across a five-page, handwritten report signed M. Leonte. I was speechless for a moment. Paduraru signed off his info reports for the Securitate using this code name! I must say that he reported objectively about what we discussed and the sites we visited. His portrayals of Rosenblum and me were laughable, nevertheless.

In his report, "Leonte" mentioned that in the village of Livezile, in the Bistrita-Nasaud County, Rosenblum bought a typewriter made in the United States, circa 1910, and paid 1,000 lei ($100 at the official rate of exchange). The typewriter was completely deteriorated after spending years buried in the ground during World War II. It was not registered with the police, "Leonte" dutifully noted.

This detail was extremely important. The rusty typewriter, past any possible use, was like a moribund political dissident: too old to be considered a threat, but still a dissident. The regime was obsessed with typewriters as much as Americans were fixated on Dracula. In my dossier, I found a dozen mentions that I was the first reporter to tackle the ultra-sensitive typewriter topic—and that pissed them off beyond imagination.

Rosenblum had bought the typewriter for his Tucson, Arizona, collection of world trinkets and souvenirs. He liked the typewriter's history: it had been buried underground and kept there for a long time, judging by its corroded looks. And it was found in close proximity of the locales described by Bram Stoker in his book.

What else did the "Leonte" source inform about? "In Sighisoara, (where in 1431 the real, not the fictional, Dracula was born) Rosenblum took many snapshots and we had lunch." The small house, right in the heart of the old medieval town, is now a bar and restaurant.

In Bistrita, at the Golden Crown Hotel where we spent the night, "on August 7th, comrade Alexandru Misiuga, director of the Bistrita County Tourism Office, offered Mort Rosenblum and Viorel Urma some *palinca* to drink and gave M. R. a table rustic lamp and a cup. M. R. in his turn offered a bottle of whisky." Wow! These were important facts, a golden trove of information for the Securitate.

Claiming that all the rooms had been booked in advance, the hosts gave Rosenblum and me a sprawling suite—usually kept for important visitors at this hotel—where "bugs" were in abundance (if not in beds then surely in the walls). Perhaps they were curious to see if we engaged in some sexual activity and wanted to catch us *in flagrante delicto*. (Being gay in Romania could draw a sentence of up to seven years in jail.) If so, they were disappointed. We slept in two detached bedrooms, separated by a bathroom and a living room, without having any visual or sonorous contact.

Comrade Misiuga, who once was formally scolded for neglecting to pay his monthly dues as a Communist Party member, was known as a huge promoter of Dracula for foreign tourists' consumption and carriers of much-needed hard currency. Whenever the Ambassadors for Friendship came from the United States on a tour of Romania, the young dancers and instrumentalists—most of them college students—stopped in Bistrita and stayed at this hotel before continuing on to the Borgo Pass and the Bran Castle.

We met a group of young Americans who were visiting through the foundation set up by Harry Morgan, a former *Reader's Digest* editor. Stories were circulating that not a few female visitors, after consuming "Dracula Elixir"—a hefty mix of Transylvanian brandy and strawberry red syrup—had been "impaled" by mutual consent on location, not by Prince Vlad of Wallachia but by their Romanian male hosts. Some were saying that Misiuga himself brought his own contribution to the pursuit of friendship and "closeness" between the United States and Romania.

Misiuga received us with open arms at the Golden Crown Hotel, just across from the Bistrita Communist Party headquarters.

Before Stoker's fictitious Jonathan Harker left Bistrita for the Borgo Pass, he dined at the Golden Crown, a mere joint compared with its socialist replica, on what locals used to call "robber steak," or bits of bacon, onion and beef seasoned with red pepper and strung on sticks and roasted over the fire.

Misiuga, an honorary member of the Dracula Society in London, compiled a dinner for Rosenblum, Paduraru and me like he did for special Dracula visitors on tour duty. The feast consisted of sandwiches with bear salami, said to increase man's sexual potency, roast beef and shish kebab, and we downed two bottles of Pinot Noir.

Capping the banquet was the biggest culinary surprise of my life: a *mamaliga* (polenta) chocolate cake. I couldn't believe my eyes when after eating away the paper-thin chocolate crust I discovered the solidified corn porridge that has nourished generations of Romanian peasants along the centuries.

"It's like taking a bride to the nuptial bed to find out she's wearing a chastity belt under her wedding gown," Misiuga quipped.

Good humored and robust, perhaps a consequence of his habit to start each day with a thick slice of salami and a small cup of elixir, Misiuga was known to Dracula fans from Tokyo to New York as the "Bear of Bistrita" because of his burly physical appearance.

He would eventually be pensioned off after frictions with the Tourism Ministry in Bucharest over his unconventional handling of the Dracula theme and his stories about the female visitors who had the pleasure to get impaled by his sharp joystick. He was forced into retirement after thirteen years (the devil's number!) as director of the Bistrita tourism office.

As far as Count Dracula was concerned, the authorities were somewhat ambivalent. They wanted the vampire to bring as many Western tourists as possible; on the other hand, they tried to make a strict delimitation between the historical truth and the fictional Dracula as depicted in Stoker's book.

The novel was banned in Romania, as were Dracula films, on the ground that they portrayed a distorted image of the real Dracula, the fifteenth-century ruler Vlad the Impaler—so-named because he impaled his Turkish enemies on stakes. Vlad was a national hero, and officials were reluctant to link him with the popular Western image of the bloodsucking count.

What did "Leonte" write in his five-page info report?

*Rosenblum criticized the poor services on the Black Sea coast and the shortages of gasoline for tourists who had to wait in line to fill up their tanks…but he said that the story "Dracula, Truth and Legend" for which he made the trip to Bistrita-Nasaud will be a positive one. We tried to demonstrate that we don't want to destroy the romanticism of the legend, which we want to keep where Bram Stoker put it, but (we don't want it) to interfere with history. Mr. Rosenblum said he convinced himself of this."*

Here is his personal opinion about Rosenblum: *"Not married. Slightly asthmatic. Jew, with sensitivities to news about Jews' fate. Moderate drinker, but a womanizer. He is aware of his power as a press man. He covers all the possible objectives."*

How did he conclude that Rosenblum was "slightly" asthmatic and a womanizer? Was it true? I had no idea. It was cheap fodder for the Securitate. "Leonte," alias Paduraru, no doubt tried to impress like a movie star.

Next there was a description of me. I almost fell off the chair with laughter:

*Type of aristocratic nature, with high opinions about his person and rather low opinions about the others. He wants to do everything by himself, because he doesn't trust the competence of other people. (He drove the car all the time; he changed the engine oil by himself.) When he drives he uses a pair of special gloves, and he waits for the other cars to allow him to pass. Impeccable behavior. Self-confidence and calm in conversation. In [the town of] Reghin he was fined for speeding [radar]. He paid the fine without commenting.*

Man, how I enjoyed "Leonte's" portrayal of my aristocratic nature and need for special gloves. Paduraru was so thorough with his details! They will remain in the Securitate annals for generations to come.

Regarding the fine for speeding, I have to say this: although they caught me in a speed trap, I had to keep my mouth shut, knowing that Paduraru would report all my comments. I didn't want to argue with the cops, and I wasn't really angry. I put the fine on my monthly expense account, so I didn't have to pay for it out of my pocket. AP did.

One day, nearly three decades after this episode, I was surprised to read this on the internet:

*Nicolae Paduraru, founder of the Transylvanian Society of Dracula, passed away on May 4, 2009, in Bucharest, Romania, after a courageous battle with cancer. Born on Dec. 6, 1937, Nicolae graduated from the University of Bucharest's English Department. He worked first as a reporter and later in the Ministry of Tourism, Department of International Relations. In 1991 he founded the Transylvanian Society of Dracula, a cultural-historical organization dedicated to scholarship and research centered on the two Draculas—the Count of Bram Stoker's novel and the fifteenth-century Wallachian voivode better known as Vlad the Impaler. In 1995, the Romanian TSD organized the first World Dracula Congress. ...Nicolae also founded the Company of Mysterious Journeys, a travel agency specializing in Dracula-themed tours. Nicolae leaves to mourn his wife and one son,*

*along with hundreds of friends, acquaintances, and tour participants*
*both in Romania and around the world.[19]*

I was really saddened by the news of Paduraru's death. He was an ed-ucated, affable, and polished person, who was very pleasant to converse with and who was very knowledgeable about world history and literature. His problem was that, through the nature of his job, he had to report his contacts with foreigners to the Securitate. If he refused to do it, he could have been demoted or fired. I am sure he had no pleasure in writing those reports, and he probably cursed the regime in his mind as everybody else did.

I am convinced that Paduraru didn't do any harm to anybody. Once, when we were passing in front of a church, I saw him crossing himself, quickly and discreetly. God rest his soul.

As for the telex from the Department of State Security in Bucharest addressed to the chief of Securitate in Constanta "please take measures for positively influencing Rosenblum Mort-Lee and for his complex control, including (the use of) special means (to monitor) his activity," I am still laughing. How can you "positively influence" an experienced journalist who reports from all corners of the world and who sees and filters everything through his own mind and eyes, no matter what the authorities want him to believe?[20]

It's a mystery to me what the knotheads from "The Eye and Ear Cooperative" meant by "complex control." The wiretaps in the walls of the *grande suite* at the Golden Crown Hotel? Paduraru's five-page written report I found in my dos-sier? The microphones hidden in the ashtrays at the restaurant? What a waste of time and effort. The Securitate had to give the illusion that they controlled everything, which was far from being the case. Most often, their means and methods were psychological. People had to believe that the Big Brother could

19 Elizabeth Miller, *Cesnur;* "Nicolae Paduraru: An Obituary," www.cesnur.org/2009/pa-duraru.htm.
20 Rosenblum's career path included a stint as executive editor for the *International Herald Tribune.* He also taught international reporting at the University of Arizona, Tucson, and has written from more than one hundred countries.

hear their words. They had to be kept insecure and in fear to prevent them from expressing their critical views of the regime. Complex control, ha. More likely complex horseshit because what I discussed with Rosenblum only the two of us knew, just as was the case with other AP visitors and colleagues. There were no witnesses around to overhear our conversations.

\* \* \*

A year after our trip to Bistrita, I left Bucharest to do a story about Hotel Tihuta, which had been recently inaugurated in the Borgo Pass, known as *Pasul Tihuta* in Romania. I had learned about it from Misiuga himself, who was very proud of his pet project—although the original plan had suffered changes. He wanted the establishment to be called Hotel Dracula, but the local Communist Party officials didn't approve it. The keepers of ideological purity also frowned on the idea of a fake graveyard next to the hotel entrance, as in Stoker's book. Instead of three towers, the hotel—seven years in the building—had only one, as the authorities wanted to economize on construction materials.

Even so, as an architectural feat, the hotel was quite a change from the usual socialist-Hiltonian types with cavernous lobbies where police informers were comfortably seated day and night, watching the human traffic. Unlike other state-owned guesthouses that had only two elevators (one of which was usually out of use), Hotel Tihuta had no elevators at all. Visitors could spend the night in a coffin, if they wanted. Few Romanians knew of the place because it was new and out of the way, located in a virgin forest on the road linking Transylvania and the northern province of Bukovina.

My first impression was that it was surreal—a surreal kitsch. The three-story hotel resembled a medieval stronghold, guarding a 3,600-foot pass where crosswinds swirled among craggy peaks—and into the lobby. The concierge's desk was on the second floor in the only tower available, and at the restaurant white-gloved waitresses served Polish vodka to local shepherds.

"I'd like to strangle the architect who built it," a long-nailed reception woman greeted me and my wife in typical Draculean fashion. Her anger was real, however, not fake. Her desk was placed in a permanent draught and with five doors opening to what was considered to be the lobby, her teeth were chattering on the cold August day.

The seventy rooms of the eerie hotel were outfitted with made-to-order furniture, which came assorted in six color patterns: red and black, white and green, and white and orange. Each client was asked when he checked in in what sort of color combination he preferred to sleep.

To make it even more Draculean, the hotel was equipped with a "torture chamber" in the basement, and Radu Varareanu, a cook, was the resident vampire. In the dimly lit chamber, there was a coffin and several skulls, which Misiuga said he had gotten for several packs of Kent cigarettes from a real cemetery in the area.

After lunch, the handful of hotel visitors was invited to the basement room where several candles were flickering. Then some of the candles snuffed out as if by magic. Our guide knocked three times on the lid of the coffin, which was swiftly removed from the inside. An apparition, covered in a black cloak stained with red paint and keeping a kitchen knife between his jaws, sprang out. The audience was terrified. I was impressed too.

The thrill was gone for vampire-cook Varareanu, who said he did the trick so often he felt like falling asleep during the wait in the coffin. Talking to the hotel hosts, I learned that an elderly woman from a group of Western visitors was recently overcome by horror and fainted when she saw the vampire jump out of the coffin with the twelve-inch long knife between his jaws.

When I went back to Bucharest, I wrote a story that got a good reception in the West, the proof being the newspaper clippings I received from Germany, Canada, and Japan. After several days I was summoned to the Tourism Ministry and reprimanded for the story. I was reminded that the figure of Wallachian ruler Vlad Tepes was "not for sale," and I was criticized for not paying enough attention to separating the historical truth from the legend. "You wrote a panegyric on Dracula and that hotel," they said. It was a bunch of baloney, of course. What had really angered them was that Radio Free Europe had broadcast the story to Romania and everybody had learned about the vampire in the coffin and the old woman who had fainted. As long as only a few Western tourists on closed circuit knew about Dracula, it was fine. But when it became a subject for a larger audience, the authorities reacted angrily: "Romania is not for sale!"

The consequences were that the coffin was removed, the "torture room" was shut down, the vampire extravaganza was banned, and cook Varareanu was fired. I knew these for facts.

Several months later, I revisited the hotel with Larry Gerber, the AP Vienna bureau chief. We had to spend a night there since we were on our way to Oradea to do a story about a Baptist church that was rumored of being in danger of demolition by the local state authorities.

When they saw me at the hotel, their faces changed. "Here you are again," the receptionist stated coldly.

"Why?" I asked.

"You don't know what happened?" she said. "You wrote an article that was broadcast by Free Europe, and that's what started the avalanche."

I then heard about Varareanu's fate, which I regret immensely. I couldn't believe that the bloodsucking count still posed a danger. The danger was magnified after Romanians began referring to Ceausescu as Vampirescu or Draculescu.

After the anti-communist revolution in 1989, the torture room was reopened for the hordes of Dracula-themed tourists, and the hotel was renamed the name that Misiuga wanted to give it originally: *Hotel Castel Dracula*.

As a token of appreciation for his lifetime achievements, Misiuga was awarded the honorary title of Baron of the House of Dracula. He died in 2009, one day before turning 85.

9

*Do you have firearms at home? One of your neighbors said he heard gunshots from the direction of your backyard.*

—QUESTION BY SECURITATE OFFICER

Bucharest
1984–85

Faced with acute economic problems and shortages of food and energy for the population, the country was sealing tight like a mussel. Ceausescu's Romania was becoming what in astronomy is called a black hole, which doesn't allow even the light to escape due to the huge gravitational pull. The gravity force was the police regime and the authorities, which a few years before had shown a certain degree of flexibility during the decade of timid liberalization that started after the mid-1960s.

I am reading a report by General Alexie Stefan, head of the Counterintelligence Directorate, addressed to his boss, Lieutenant-General Iulian Vlad, in which he asks for permission to open a special surveillance file to gather evidence "for [Urma's] slandering[21] in view of his removal from his job." It added: "Simultaneously, we will act to determine him to give up the writing and sending of news unfavorable to the Socialist Republic of Romania."

Vlad, who would play an interesting role in the 1989 anti-Ceausescu uprising by quickly and graciously switching sides and allegiances in the best Romanian tradition, answered that, "Of course, he must be kept under surveillance, but why didn't you do this immediately after suspicions were raised?"

---

21 Otherwise known as character assassination.

In a firm and angry tone, Vlad continued in his written address, which I found attached at page 144 of my Securitate dossier:

"Thoroughly analyze this case, and draw the necessary conclusions and lessons regarding the inefficient way in which you understood to act for prevention.

"Why did you take notice so late about the lack of permission [to open the *DUI* surveillance file]? Why didn't you act immediately after he started to denigrate? Why did you wait so long? Check the situation of other press correspondents in this category," Vlad thundered. He must have been livid.

I agree with Vlad on this. Why did they wait so long? I was "denigrating" the revolutionary conquests of Romania, and nothing was happening to me. I was still walking freely? No bones crushed? Why so late? I thought, "Search me, comrade general, I don't know. I said before that all of you were a bunch of incompetent bozos that were good at using the stick, but you lacked the intelligence and finesse to handle more subtle situations. You were good at torturing Kirschen and making him walk barefoot in circles for four days and four nights in a tiny cell until you forced him to 'confess.' You did a great job of kicking Gheorghe Ursu—a critic of the regime—in the stomach and beating him to death while he was in the custody of the Securitate and police. And you did the same to thousands of others like him. You did a fantastic job at brutalizing and persecuting the perceived opponents of the totalitarian state."

I was admonished in one of the Securitate notes on page 145 in my dossier, dated May 17, 1984, that—despite the warning by the Agerpres management—I was still displaying a "hostile attitude" and publishing "articles with unfavorable content for RS Romania." On the note, General Vlad had scribbled, "Execute the order of comrade Minister secretary of state T. Postelnicu. The 3rd Directorate should finalize the case, as was established with comrade Minister [of foreign affairs] Stefan Andrei. Signed Lt. Gen. I. Vlad."

Now comrade Andrei was getting involved, discussing my situation with comrade Vlad. I don't know what comrade Postelnicu's order was.

He was in charge of the Interior Ministry. At the time that these things happened, I had no idea what was going on. I was not aware that officials paid so much attention to my person. True, I was the only Romanian citizen who was working for a Western news medium. As I mentioned earlier, Reuters and France Presse also wanted to hire Romanians, but the authorities did not give them permission to work, and the two agencies had refused to accept the Romanians that Agerpres presented to them.

I was the first and the last Romanian correspondent. The authorities could not have imagined that things would get so bad when they grudgingly gave me the approval in 1975, and now they didn't know how to proceed without setting off an international scandal. That's why the Securitate felt the need to talk to Andrei, the foreign minister. "What shall we do, comrade minister? What methods can we use? Carrots or sticks? Sorry, but we are somewhat short of carrots." They banned me from writing and sending stories, but that was all they could do. They were waiting to see how things would play out. As an Agerpres senior manager had said several years before, "When Urma will stop being a correspondent, his future won't be too rosy." They were waiting to see how the AP would react. Then they would decide how rosy my future would be. Meanwhile, I was getting more and more phone calls from anonymous voices that were cursing and threatening me.

"Awwwooooo," they would imitate the howl of a wolf, "Awwwooooo, traitor...son of a bitch...Judas...expletives. Awwwooooo!"

The Securitate had a large zoo, and the "wolves" seemed hungry, but fortunately, in my case they were only howling and not biting.

There had been a steady decrease in the Romanians' living standard between 1980 and 1989, when the *Conducator* was toppled in a confused bloody revolution. To pay for his ill-conceived industrialization plans (the country produced more steel than Great Britain per person!), Ceausescu borrowed heavily from the West, but these loans ultimately ravaged the country's finances. To remedy this he decided to pay off Romania's foreign debt as fast as possible—and at all costs. He ordered the export of much of the country's agricultural and industrial production, resulting in domestic shortages, which made Romanians' everyday life a fight for survival. Food rationing was introduced, and heating, gas, and electricity blackouts became the rule. While the country was going through extremely difficult times with long bread lines in front of empty food stores, Ceausescu was often shown on state TV entering stores jam-packed with food supplies and praising the "high living standard" achieved under his rule. Romania had become not only a "black hole" but also a Potemkin village.

Even Elena Ceausescu felt the need to contribute to her husband's savings campaign for paying off the foreign debt. One day she had the idea to cut Agerpres's budget and stop the payments in Romanian currency and in dollars that the agency made to international news agencies for the exchange of news and photos. They were not terminating the contracts. They simply didn't want to pay anymore. Maybe she thought that Agerpres would continue to get the news services free. Perhaps she thought, "We can fool the rich capitalists!" It was not the case. The result was that all the Western news agencies stopped their news streams (via Budapest and Belgrade) to Romania.

"If there is so much talk in the West about the free flow of information, why should we spend our dollars to get news from capitalists? It should be free," she was reported to have said. Apparently she didn't know that the "free flow" had a political and not a financial connotation.

I was on speaking terms with a handful of Agerpres editors who told me that the decision had been a serious blow, leaving government institutions, such as the Foreign Ministry, without much knowledge of what was going in the world. They had to give up the compilation of the daily bulletins for *uz intern* (closed-circuit use) intended for the information of the country's leadership. The bulletins were replacing a lack of information from Romania's embassies abroad that had to trim their staffs to comply with the budget cuts Elena ordered. There was no other Soviet-bloc country that had cut its flow of international information. Isolated and loathed, Romania was sealing tight like a mussel.

Along with the Associated Press, Agerpres had an extensive contract for the exchange of both news and photos. When Ceausescu traveled overseas, his photos were immediately transmitted back to Romania—not by flying pigeons but through AP's vast photo network.

As tightfisted as they were when meeting with AP every two or three years to renew and pay a little more for their news contract, when Ceausescu went abroad, there was no bargaining. The Romanian leader was traveling in style, with suitcases overflowing with dollars, and he was willing to pay cash—no matter how much—without grumbling. AP, however, never charged his entourage more than the agency did with its other customers in similar situations.

\* \* \*

One day I received a visit from two plainclothesmen who flashed their Securitate ID cards before my eyes, and said they'd like to talk to me. It was past noon, and I was at home where I usually went for lunch before returning to the office. "Please do come in," I said politely. One of them asked me abruptly if I was in possession of firearms.

"Geez," I told myself, "these guys don't waste their time with gracious introductions. They don't mince words."

"Firearms?" I asked aloud. "God forbid. Why are you asking?"

"One of your neighbors said that he heard gunshots from the direction of your backyard," said the other plainclothes officer.

"I don't have any. Never had," I answered.

"Not even a hunting rifle?"

"No, not even that," I said firmly.

"Did you do some repair work recently? Did you 'shoot' the walls to hang your paintings?" said the first, casting a circular look around the room.

"The most recent repairs we made were after the big quake in 1977. Since then, nothing," I answered.

"Perhaps one of your neighbors made repairs. The 'shots' must have come from them," said the other, attempting to attenuate the seriousness of the question and to change the subject. Having a gun and hiding it from authorities was almost equivalent to capital murder.

"What do they want from me?" I was thinking. I was trying hard to find an answer. They wanted to intimidate me, for sure. But what was the real purpose of their visit?

"Listen," said one of them. "Do you have Persian rugs, stylish furniture, and valuable paintings?"

"I have what you can see. This is my parents' home. My father was a mechanical engineer; now he is retired. My mother was a homemaker, and she raised my brother and me. There wasn't enough money left for Persian rugs and expensive furniture. Why are you asking?"

"Well…you know…we received a letter from one of your neighbors in which he says you have all the things we mentioned."

"Can you give me a name?" I asked incredulously.

"No, it's not signed. It's an anonymous letter."

"Do you take unsigned letters seriously? Anybody can claim anything in them; what's their importance?"

"They are important because we can learn something if we investigate. They don't tell the truth 100 per cent, but some things can be useful for us to know," said one of them, laughing. I thought, "So that's why you came—to see what I have in my home. Perhaps the anonymous letter was just a pretext."

"Can we ask you a favor? Can we look around, if you don't mind?" said the other. I was expecting this.

"Not at all. Go ahead," I answered. I breathed easily. If they saw what was in the house, then the idea of expensive paintings and rugs would quickly get out of their heads. I took them to the bedrooms on the second floor to see with their own eyes, and they asked me to open the wardrobes. No problem! At the end I asked them what they intended to do.

"We'll write a report—a reply to the anonymous letter we received. We'll say that the things mentioned are not true. This solves the problem," they said.

In the middle of the dining room table was a pack of BT cigarettes in a fruit vase. "Do you mind if we take one?" asked one of them, a little embarrassed. The temptation was too big. The Bulgarian cigarettes were superior to anything that the domestic market produced.

"You can take the whole pack. My father is a smoker. I'm not," I said.

"No, that's fine; we'll take one for each of us. It's enough. Thank you."
They left.

I could have said no when they asked me for permission to look around the house. They didn't come with a search warrant, after all. But why complicate things when I had nothing to hide? You want to see what's in the rooms and wardrobes? No problem. You can also check the bathroom to see if the toilet flushes OK. You can pull the chain. It's working!

When my wife came home from work, she got scared.

"What if they came to put microphones in the house? Have you been with them all the time?"

"Yes, with the exception of five or six minutes when I had to prepare lunch, and they were writing their report on the dining table…"

"Check the table; go under it to see that they didn't hide anything," my wife said. I did what she told me to do, but there was nothing there. They didn't come to install microphones. I thought that listening devices were already in the house, at least in the room where the AP teleprinter had been installed, and they had to extend all sorts of wires to connect it to the electric pole outside.

It turned out that I was right, as I read in their reports attached to my dossier and as I found years later in the walls of the house. The authorities acknowledged that they never thought that one day I (as millions of other Romanians) would be able to see my file.

"For documenting and halting the hostile activity unfolded by URMA SERGIU VIOREL, in the process of evidence gathering…*special measures were carried out at the home of the objective*, as well as the office of the 'Associated Press' agency where he unfolds his professional activity," the Securitate said about the decision to open the special surveillance dossier for me, the one described as a "superior form of monitoring." I would have a dossier within a dossier, as I already had a regular file.

My superiors were not happy with the authorities' decision to freeze my reporting about Romania and withdraw my accreditation. Here is the text of a letter Thomas Fenton, the director of the Central and East Europe Bureau in Frankfurt, sent to the Ministry of Foreign Affairs, as I found it in my dossier:

*29.10.1985*
*Gheorghe Gustea*
*Chief of Press*
*Ministry of Foreign Affairs*

*Dear Mr. Gustea,*

*Mr. Viorel Urma, who has been the AP correspondent in Bucharest for more than ten years, tells me that questions have arisen concerning his status and that it is not clear he will be able to continue his work. I'm very distressed and surprised about this. Mr. Urma is one of our best correspondents, and it would be a serious setback for the AP if he were unable to work as a journalist...Would you be kind enough to clarify the situation for me."*

Leafing through my dossier, I found at page 295 a two-page letter sent by Romania's embassy in Washington to the Ministry of Foreign Affairs in Bucharest, after a meeting between Ambassador Nicolae Gavrilescu and Roland Kuchel, director of the Office of East European and Yugoslav Affairs at the US Department of State. Here it is verbatim and in its entirety:

*MINISTRY OF FOREIGN AFFAIRS*

*TELEGRAM*                                    *SECRET*
                                              *U[rgent]*

*WASHINGTON*                    *074135 09.11.1985/19,00*

*We inform you that director Roland Kuchel made an appeal at our embassy similar to the one made several days ago at MFA by the cultural counselor of the US Embassy in Bucharest in connection with the ceasing of activity of Associated Press correspondent Viorel Urma.*

*Kuchel stressed from very beginning that this is not a protest of the American side, since it's about the sovereign act of the Romanian authorities regarding the ceasing of activity of a Romanian citizen. That's why he raises this issue with the plea that it should be solved in the spirit of the good relations between the two countries, including the press domain.*

*In essence, Kuchel said the State Department supports the request of the Associated Press management (which sent a letter in this regard to our embassy) that Romania's competent authorities revisit their initial decision and allow Viorel Urma to resume his activity as a correspondent of the agency. Kuchel said that the Associated Press management was pleased with Urma's professional activity, who along 10 years of activity had sent correct information about Romania that contributed to a better understanding in the USA of the situation in our country. That's why, he said, the decision regarding the ceasing of Viorel Urma's activity without an explanation or without reproaching him anything, was like a shock for the Associated Press management. The definitive ceasing of his activity would be a great loss for the Associated Press, depriving it of the possibility to have stories about Romania from the sources of a local correspondent, since for financial reasons it would not be possible for the agency to send an American correspondent to Bucharest.*

*The State Department supports the Associated Press proposal to dispatch immediately a representative to Bucharest to rediscuss this issue.*

*In this context, talking about certain difficulties some American reporters had met in their relations with us, [Kuchel] mentioned the situation of Bradley Graham from the Washington Post, who was denied an entrance visa and that of Henry Kamm from the New York Times, who was advised by Agerpres about the way he should write about Romania. Kuchel admitted that sometimes some journalists push things too far and don't adopt a constructive attitude.*

*[Romania] however should not cut the dialogue with them so that they don't join the hostile voices. Kuchel stressed that a positive decision of the Romanian authorities in connection with the Associated Press correspondent would have a favorable echo in the American press circles taking into account the influential position of the Associated Press agency especially in the context of the upcoming visit to Bucharest of Secretary of State Shultz.*

*In connection with problems stated by Kuchel regarding Viorel Urma, he was told that his situation is not known at our embassy and that the MAE [Ministerul Afacerilor Externe] will be informed.*

*During the conversation it was reaffirmed the position of the Romanian authorities toward foreign journalists, including those from the USA, and [our] interest of developing direct relations with those journalists who show an objective attitude in their materials about Romania's realities and policies, who don't come to this country with preconceived ideas only to write disparaging and purely speculative materials, deliberately ignoring the positive aspects.*

*(Ambassador) Nicolae Gavrilescu*

At the bottom of the first page was this notation: "This information was sent to comrades Constantin Mitea, Alexandru Ionescu, Iulian Vlad, Aristotel Stamatoiu, and Ion Ghenoiu." Gavrilescu sent his telegram, as he called it, to a select group of Romanian senior officials. Mitea was one of Ceausescu's counselors, Ionescu was the editor-in-chief of the Communist Party paper *Scanteia*, Stamatoiu was chief of DIE (the Romanian CIA), and Ghenoiu was head of the Passport Department, with the rank of general.

After only four days, the generals were sharing Gavrilescu's telegram among themselves, trying to find a way out of the problem.

This is what I came across in my dossier, after Vlad passed on the ambassador's letter to one of his deputies:

*Comrade General Mortoiu*
*For your information and for measures.*

*General Iulian Vlad*
*13.11.1985*

What kind of measures were they talking about? Aurelian Mortoiu was the head of the Counterintelligence Directorate in 1985. This time Vlad seemed impassive and less involved than when he ordered, "Thoroughly analyze this case and draw the necessary conclusions and lessons regarding the inefficient way in which you understood to act for prevention… Why didn't you act immediately after he started to denigrate?"

Was this the signal that after the AP and the State Department intervention, the Securitate felt compelled to soften its accusing voice? Perhaps this was the right conclusion. After this exchange, and until I left Romania, no Securitate officer would call me or pay a visit to the AP office in Bucharest. They became invisible, but at that time I had no explanation for their lack of interest regarding my person. Undoubtedly, they were still watching me.

* * *

As promised, AP dispatched Vienna bureau chief Larry Gerber to meet with Gheorghe Gustea, a counselor in the Press and Culture Department of the Foreign Ministry. When Gerber asked him the reasons for which my press accreditation had been cancelled, Gustea said that I had never been accredited as an AP correspondent. The Romanian authorities considered me a "technical-administrative representative with limited rights in supporting" the visiting AP reporters.

Gustea said that as time went on I had gone "beyond my responsibilities by transmitting news and stories…with a negative content." He said that the "Romanian side would be ready to present two or three candidates from which AP could choose a local correspondent."

Nice! You know what? Screw you, "Romanian side." Keep your Securitate people for other situations; don't try to infiltrate them among American reporters.

They considered me a correspondent only if I was reproducing what Agerpres was saying about "the grandiose Golden Epoch of the Best Son of the Nation, the Danube of Wisdom, the Genius of the Carpathians," comrade Nicolae Ceausescu. Hurrah!

If I was writing stories with a "negative content" I was not a correspondent any longer.

Irked by the Romanian's explanation, the State Department had a new intervention a week after the meeting between Gerber and Gustea.

I read this on page 295 in my dossier:

*Ministry of Foreign Affairs*
*Directia Relatii V*
*Nr. 5/2513*

## MEETING RECORD

*On November 18, 1985, Ion Besteliu, acting director of Directia Relatii V [North America Department] received the visit of Nuel Pazdral, political counselor of the USA Embassy in Bucharest.*

*Referring to the discussions which Frank Strovas, press and culture counselor of the USA Embassy, had with officials from the Press and Culture Department of the Ministry of Foreign Affairs and Agerpres concerning Viorel Urma, a Romanian citizen hired by Associated Press, N. Pazdral said that while "Associated Press is ready to further pursue this matter," the American embassy is concerned by the effects this problem can have in the process of the renewal of the most-favored nation clause and by the possible reaction of the Western press in connection with the increase of the press control in [Romania].*

*In addition, this can be interpreted as an attempt by the Romanian government to diminish the flow of information to the USA.*

*[Pazdral] mentioned that it's difficult for the Associated Press management to understand why the Romanian side refuses to accredit Urma as a correspondent, when he "transmitted correct information" to the Associated Press agency for 10 years.*

*Ion Besteliu took note of what was communicated and said that this is not a political problem but a technical one, which falls under the jurisdiction of Agerpres. In addition, V. Urma was never accredited as a correspondent of Associated Press, and if the agency wants to hire a Romanian press correspondent it can discuss this with Agerpres, which will present a number of candidates [...]*

*The meeting lasted forty minutes.*

# 10

*We all agree that at this moment nobody needs headaches...*

—From my letter to Mircea Raceanu

Bucharest
Winter 1985–Fall 1987

I was free, but isolated. I didn't know what was going on. Nobody had told me about Kuchel's visit to the Romanian embassy in Washington and the meetings between Strovas and Pazdral with Foreign Ministry officials in Bucharest.

I was not communicating with the US Embassy, and I was unaware of their intercessions to ask the authorities to lift the writing ban. They seemed better informed than I was about the Securitate reports, and I had little doubt that they had their own sources of information within the regime.

I was only aware of the meetings between the government officials and my superiors in Vienna and Frankfurt. When they came to Bucharest, I did not accompany them as an interpreter anymore. Officials told me, "We have our own translators, thank you"—meaning, "Screw you; get lost."

Before the visit of Secretary of State George Shultz to Romania in December 1985, Larry Gerber, the Vienna bureau chief, met with Romanian diplomats to discuss US-Romanian relations—and to find out if there were any changes regarding my status. He met with Mircea Raceanu, head of the diplomacy department responsible for relations with all the countries of the Americas.

I had met Raceanu before when my colleagues from bureaus in Europe came on other visits. What impressed me was his open and friendly way.

He was cut from a different cloth than other Romanian diplomats. I had met ambassadors Valentin Lipatti and Corneliu Bogdan, and they had an arrogant air and looked down on me. In fact they ignored my presence in the room. Raceanu was a stark contrast. Apart from being affable and relaxed, he was speaking a different language than the other diplomats-bureaucrats. He had more substance and offered reporters more information and quotes, not only the boring stuff from Ceausescu's playbook. Raceanu had something that made him more credible.[22]

I asked Larry to give him a letter in which I explained my situation and my decision to emigrate and join my brother in the United States. This seemed to be the most effective solution for both sides. I was convinced that they wouldn't change their mind and reconsider the status of my accreditation. However, I was not sure that Raceanu would accept it. While Larry talked to him, I was waiting in the office car in the parking lot. When he came back, he said that Raceanu had read the letter and put it in his pocket. I was greatly surprised.

I found a photocopy of the English original and its translation into Romanian in my dossier. In essence, I told him that despite my efforts to be as accurate and objective as possible, I had run into problems with the authorities and that they no longer considered me a correspondent. I also informed him about my decision to leave the country and my request for the issuance of a passport of a Romanian citizen with foreign residency. I didn't want to be stripped of my Romanian citizenship because, with such a passport, I could travel as an AP reporter wherever the agency would send me.

---

22  In 1989, Raceanu was accused of being involved in espionage for the United States since the mid-1970s when he was a secretary in the Embassy of Romania in Washington. In an interview with the *New York Times* in 1990, he said he gave information on human rights and religious freedom. "I never betrayed Romania or Romanian national interests [...] I betrayed Ceausescu personally and his policy, which was basically against Romania and the Romanian people." He was sentenced to death, but he was freed from prison during the Romanian revolution. Soon after his release, he left the country and settled in the United States.
(David Binder, "A Ceausescu Political Prisoner Says He Betrayed Ex-Ruler, Not Country," *The New York Times*, January 8, 1990)

I did not get an answer from him or other officials, but this had not been my purpose. At least now, they knew of my plans. Give me a passport and a valid exit visa and good-bye. It was the most diplomatic way to "halt my hostile activity." However, they didn't seem enchanted with my idea.

(In his *New York Times* interview, Raceanu said that he had assisted a number of Romanians who were having trouble obtaining exit visas. I doubt that I was one of them, although I am certain that he talked about my case with US diplomats)

During his visit, Secretary of State Shultz warned Ceausescu that Romania would be deprived of the most-favored nation trade treatment (and lose billions of dollars as a consequence) if Bucharest did not improve its human-rights record.

After Shultz, no senior member of the Reagan cabinet would visit Romania until Ceausescu's downfall. In October 1988—during a visit by John Whitehead, a deputy state secretary—Ceausescu complained about the "ideological" position of the Reagan administration, unfavorably comparing it with the Nixon administration. Gone was the time when Ceausescu and Nixon were singing each other's praises.

I am reading in my dossier (page 313) a report with proposals to close my individual surveillance dossier, which the Securitate had opened for the "clarification of suspicions of treason in favor of the American information service..." It was dated January 19, 1986, with the remark "approved [...] the action ends immediately" and was signed illegibly by a general. It was two months after Roland Kuchel's visit to the Romanian Embassy in Washington and a month after Raceanu had accepted my letter.

I had no idea why they closed the special *DUI* surveillance dossier, which was part of the bigger, general surveillance dossier. Perhaps they wanted to avoid diplomatic complications. The most-favored nation trading clause that was granted to Romania in 1975 was very dear to Ceausescu. It had to be renewed annually after a Congressional review of the country's human-rights record. Ceausescu played a silly game. Each year he opened the door of the cage that was Romania for one or two months, allowing the "birds" to fly to the West. After Congress approved the temporary extension, Ceausescu, the bird catcher, slammed shut the door of the cage for another year.

After I informed the authorities of my decision to emigrate, I formally applied for a passport, together with my wife and our six-year-old son. However, obtaining it was not easy. I had to wait more than a year; my first application was turned down, and I had to reapply.

As I said, the Securitate had stopped their visits to our office, and at that time I had no explanation for the change. I didn't know they had closed my dossier, as I was unaware that they had opened one in the first place.

However the "anonymous" phone calls, both at home and at the office, didn't stop. What was intriguing was that after I put the phone back in the fork, the line was still open, and the voice at the other end continued to bad-mouth me until the speaker got bored. Once I slammed down the receiver, and after I lifted it a minute later, the voice was still belittling me, without pause. How advanced were the "organs" in their audio techniques!

In the spring of 1987, Mikhail Gorbachev came to Romania: the Eastern-bloc nation thought to be the least susceptible to his idea of *glasnost* (openness) and *perestroika* (restructuring). Ceausescu had not taken kindly to suggestions that his country follow the Soviet lead in introducing reform and liberalization. Romanian officials claimed that they had embraced Soviet-style, economic reforms and self-management years before the Kremlin.

The Securitate was mobilized to avoid any incidents involving ordinary citizens and critics of the regime or officials who were viewed as Russophiles. The foreign reporters who were accredited for the visit were kept under surveillance around the clock. I did not receive the press accreditation, as was expected, but our office car was tailed from morning until night, when I parked it at home.

To cover the visit, the AP sent Alison Smale, the new Vienna bureau chief, who had worked for the agency in Moscow for several years and knew all the nooks and crannies of the system. She went everywhere that the journalists had access and reported about the talks between Gorbachev and Ceausescu.[23] I spent most of the time at the office, contributing with information about the Romanians' daily problems and their reaction to the visit. Unlike the Soviet Union, the country was not heading toward reform but toward austerity. The crisis Romania was facing was mainly due to the *Conducator's* foolish decision to pay off the foreign debt as fast as he could and at any cost to the Romanians.

I was also trying to check reports about the appearance on Bucharest's streets of "freedom dogs." These were said to be stray dogs that were seen roaming the streets in a residential district, dressed in men's shirts on which had been written "Down with Ceausescu" and "We want Gorbachev." In panic, the authorities rushed uniformed and plainclothes police to catch the dissident pets and their owners. The cops spread poison in the area, and together with the five or six canine political activists, scores of other innocent mongrels were killed in the crackdown. The owners of the shirts were never caught.

Thinking about pro-Gorbachev sympathizers, I had the idea to contact Ion Iliescu, who had fallen from Ceausescu's graces along the years and was now a humble director of *Editura Tehnica*. But where was Iliescu? Each time I called his office, his secretary told me that "comrade Iliescu" was very busy. Busy, busy, busy. Most likely he was lying low, to avoid meeting with foreign reporters. Rumors were flying that he had been ordered to leave Bucharest for the duration of Gorbachev's visit. Everybody knew that he would replace Ceausescu when the time came. Nobody knew when that time would come though.

Iliescu, a cunning and wily politician, was waiting patiently for his transformation from a small fish to a presidential shark, and he kept a low profile. He avoided reporters and pro-Moscow former officials who had been demoted and had joined the opposition ranks—a very weak opposition, honestly speaking. It was more of a collection of isolated voices of ex-apparatchiks, such as Gheorghe Apostol and Silviu Brucan, who

---

23
Google search:
Alison Smale "Romania Cool Toward Gorbachev's First Visit," May 25, 1987.
Alison Smale "Gorbachev Visit Gives Romania First Dose of Glasnost," May 27, 1987.
Alison Smale "Gorbachev Voices Muted Criticism of Ties with Romania," May 26, 1987.

had enjoyed all the advantages of the communist regime before. Again, it is hard to understand why Ceausescu did not attempt to get rid of Iliescu. Maybe he was afraid of Moscow's reaction. Two things scared the Romanian leader the most: Moscow and Washington. He couldn't escape the consequences in both instances. In 1988 the US Congress would withdraw the MFN status as a measure of retribution for the continued emigration restrictions and human-rights violations, which led to the breakdown of special ties that existed between the two countries. In addition, Moscow—with Washington's consent—would play a crucial role in Ceausescu's overthrow one year later.

Meanwhile, I had reapplied for the right to emigrate after my first petition was rejected by the Passport Department—which was run by the Interior Ministry, home of the Securitate secret police and the regular police force. There was no other way out. My wife had been fired from her job as a schoolteacher as she was not considered a "positive model" for the younger generations. The superintendent of the school district tried to discourage her from accompanying me to the West. "If you leave and your mother has a traffic accident, won't you regret it?" she said. My wife was incensed, but she resisted the psychological pressure and blackmail.

Waiting for an answer, I sold our office car, "the Swan of the Balkans," and deposited the money into the AP account, which was almost depleted. In June 1987, I was told that my petition for a passport and exit visa had been approved. This happened right before Congress opened discussions for the extension of the trading clause for another year. Ceausescu had to unlock the door of the cage for those wishing to leave the country, before shutting it tight a short time after.

I did an inventory of the office—including furniture and teleprinter, but minus the wiretaps in the walls—and sent it to our financial service in Frankfurt. I sealed the office…and until January 1990, the AP would cease to have anybody in Romania. When we came back after the revolution, we wouldn't find anything—not even the office, as a physical entity. Everything we had there had been removed and put in a government warehouse for storage, and the studio apartment was rented to somebody else after the building renovation—even though we continued to pay rent for it for some time.[24]

In October 1987, my wife, our son, and I boarded a Tarom flight with Vienna as our destination. I was infinitely more fortunate than Kirschen, who spent ten years in prison before they let him go to London. Perhaps this was one of the reasons that they didn't "cook my hide" as they did his. I had to put up with crude means of psychological intimidation, such as phoned-in threats and expletives, but they didn't touch me physically. I have no doubts that they regretted that they were constrained to verbal abuse only, leaving the sticks for other situations. My wife said I had somebody "up there" who protected me. Maybe I have a lucky star.

I was leaving behind my eighty-two-year-old father, a happy and carefree boyhood, the house in which I was born, and all my memories until that time—which will follow me for the rest of my life, wherever I am.

After three years at the AP bureau in Vienna, covering and editing stories about Eastern Europe, I would get to New York —the end of my journey across two continents.

I'd like to mention the AP reporters with whom I worked in Romania when they came for short visits to cover major political events or to do feature stories. We got along very well, and they were my friends. They were my messengers to the free world, and I often think of them fondly. I learned a lot from each of them, and I valued their advice and collegiality. Isolated as I was, their visits were the only occasions for me to speak English. Those reporters are: Nick Ludington, Otto Doelling, Steve Miller, Denis Gray, Robert Reid, Larry Gerber, Alexander Higgins, George Jahn, Alison Smale,[25] Dave Minthorn, Ken Jautz, Mort Rosenblum, and Hugh Mulligan.

I cannot end this chapter without mentioning the "blue-eyed boys" from the 3rd Directorate of Counterintelligence—who looked after me

---

24 The seven-story building at 30 Corbeni Street, Sector 2, where the AP office was located in Bucharest between 1975 and 1987 was torn down in the 1990s to make room for Hotel Monte Nelly.

25 Smale, a British journalist, would later become the executive editor of the *International Herald Tribune*, making her the first woman to be in charge of the paper.

exemplarily and whose names I found in my dossier. I am still in awe of the work they did to put together so many pages: Lt. Col. H. Salamanian, Col. Dan Marinescu, Cpt. Ilie Gheorghe, Lt. Col. Bucur Gheorghe, Lt. Col. Gheorghe Diaconescu, Lt. Col. Moise Orban, Maj. Leon Gheorghiu, Lt. Maj. Muresan P., Cpt. Stanescu Gabriel, Cpt. Camarasan Ioan, Maj. Stoian Gheorghe, Cpt. Soare Ion—plus four generals, Gheorghe Zagoneanu, Iulian Vlad, Alexie Stefan, and Aurelian Mortoiu.

To all of you, who are still dragging your worthless carcasses on the streets of our homeland or who are buried in the cemeteries of our homeland, two words: Get stuffed!

From the headquarters of the National Council for the Study of the Securitate Archives, after reading my Dossier No. 223442, I want to share a bit of sarcasm: Great job, guys. Congratulations!

\* \* \*

Shortly before I left, the makeshift arch of triumph made of pressed cardboard and wood at the entrance of the Exhibition Complex which bore the legend "The Golden Epoch – The Epoch of Nicolae Ceausescu" burned down one night, and unable to catch the anti-regime arsonists, the police blamed "an accumulation of heat during the summer" for the mysterious blaze. Eventually, as a popular joke went on, the culprits were caught after Lenin, his sculpted glare beaming condorlike from the pedestal in the *Piata Scanteii* square across from the Exhibition Complex, saw who the criminals were and reported them to the police.

Neither Lenin escaped "unpunished." Several months after the 1989 revolution, the 10-ton statue was toppled, spat at, kicked and booed by the furious masses. In 2004 when I visited Romania, Lenin was lying on his back in the grass and gazing at the stars in the vast tree park of the seventeenth-century Mogosoaia Palace just outside Bucharest, while several youths appeared to have a good time making jokes and jumping on the vandalized statue. The great leader of the world's proletariat enjoyed the same fate in the other satellite-states of the Soviet Union after the fall of the Iron Curtain.

# 11

*Welcome to the outside! It's been a long struggle, and I'm delighted you and family have finally made it safely.*

—LARRY HEINZERLING, DEPUTY DIRECTOR OF AP WORLD
SERVICES, AT MY ARRIVAL IN VIENNA

Vienna
Winter 1989

"**D**udes, we've won! The dictator has fled."
On December 22, 1989, I was listening to Radio Bucharest, which was the only source of official information—or disinformation—I had of what was going on in Romania. I had been in the AP bureau in Vienna for more than two years, where I was writing and editing stories from Eastern Europe, which was boiling like a volcano. The communist regimes had already been swept from power in Poland, Czechoslovakia, Hungary, East Germany, and Bulgaria, and now it was Romania's turn.

It was shortly before noon, and I was keeping my ears glued to the radio, which offered a mélange of Party songs and news bulletins during the morning. Unexpectedly, the station went off the air, and the transistor went dead. I thought that poor reception was to blame. I picked up the phone, and I called my colleagues from Radio Free Europe in Munich, asking them if they knew what was happening in Bucharest. They didn't know more than what I already knew. It was only by listening to RFE the week before that I was able to know what was happening in Timisoara, the city in western Romania that was the cradle and the spark of the anti-Ceausescu uprising.

After the AP bureau was shut down, there were no Western reporters in Romania to do spot stories. The regime had stopped giving entry visas to foreign journalists,[26] the only exception being for those accredited to cover the 14th Congress of the Romanian Communist Party, which ended without surprises: the *Conducator* was reelected unanimously for another five-year term.

Romania had become a perfect "black hole." Nobody entered and nobody was able to escape to the West—except for gymnast Nadia Comaneci, who fled to Austria. She illegally crossed the border into neighboring Hungary one November night on her way to freedom, climbing seven barbed-wire fences, much to the authorities' humiliation.

"I'd trudged through freezing water and across icy fields and climbed over barbed-wire fences, all the while expecting to be shot," she recalled in her 2003 memoir, *Letters to a Young Gymnast.*

All of a sudden, the radio came back to life, and I heard a voice—strangled by emotion and against a cacophonous background of other voices—screaming: "Dudes, we've won! The dictator has fled." The voice belonged to Mircea Dinescu, a poet and regime critic.

What had seemed impossible until then became incredible all of a sudden. Could it be true? Overcome by emotion and with my heart seeming like it would pound out of my chest, I hollered, "Ceausescu is kaput! I heard it on Radio Bucharest, which is government controlled." Perhaps from that very moment it had stopped being one of the regime's mouthpieces.

Alison Smale, the bureau chief, stopped editing a story from Prague, and in ten seconds she wrote and rushed a bulletin with the news that went round the globe in less than a minute. We were the first to alert the world to the event.

---

26 Compare this with about forty foreign journalists, most of them from England and the United States, who were roaming the Balkans and reporting from Bucharest in 1940 before Romania joined Nazi Germany in invading the Soviet Union to recapture Bessarabia. Among those journalists were Cyrus Sulzberger from the *New York Times*, Cedric Salter from the *Daily Mail*, Clare Hollingworth from the *Sunday Times*, Robert St. John from AP, and Frank Stevens from the United Press. Their home base was the Athénée Palace.

"Keep listening," she said. "Tell us what else is going on. We'll do the story and slap your byline on it."

The radio was broadcasting live from the main TV studio saying that the headquarters of the Party Central Committee had been taken by assault and penetrated by the thousands of protesters gathered in *Piata Palatului*, the vast square in front of the former royal palace. In the hullabaloo that dominated the event, there were cries of "Victory! We've won! The Army is with us!" and "Ceausescu has fled!" Ceausescu had been rescued by an Army helicopter from the roof of the building to save him from being lynched by the furious mob and had left Bucharest for an unknown destination. I was translating and communicating what I was hearing to Alison, and she wrote and filed the breaking news and terse dispatches from her computer. It became evident that this was the beginning of the end for Ceausescu and his dictatorship.

"Keep your calm. God has turned his face toward Romania." I heard Dinescu's voice, as he was addressing Romanians from the TV studio, surrounded by electrified revolutionaries from all occupations. His words marked my mind and soul. God had given a big favor to us, but how would Romanians answer his gesture?

In 1989 Romania was a gloomy and depressed nation. The people were physically and psychologically undermined by food shortages and the cold in their homes in winter, and they had been brought to desperation by the austerity and the lack of prospects for a better life. It was a country where even the right to hope had been confiscated.

My colleagues asked me many times how I foresaw the end of communism in Romania. "It will be a bloody mess," I told them, and they were surprised to hear me say this. I explained. "The Ceausescu regime is the harshest in the Soviet bloc. Under him, the Securitate was one of the most brutal secret police forces in the world, responsible for the arrest, torture, and deaths of thousands of people. They won't give up power peacefully and willingly. Romania is not Czechoslovakia, and there will be no 'velvet revolution' here. The Securitate controls everything. It will fight to the end to support the tyrant and the system. Why would they agree to lose their advantages? Apart from that, all the mass movements in Romania's history ended in bloodshed. It will be chaos, tears, and suffering."

I was right—but only partially. I never thought that the Securitate and the army would abandon Ceausescu so quickly. In the end, there was an easy explanation for all that happened.

The hungry and desperate crowds started an anti-Ceausescu regime revolution on the morning of December 22, but toward the evening it turned into a coup led by the pro-Soviet faction in the Communist Party. This was a plan that Ion Iliescu, Silviu Brucan, Virgil Magureanu, Army General Nicolae Militaru, and others had worked out.

Firmly backed by the Securitate, Iliescu would abandon the "pickling" jar where Ceausescu had put him as director of *Editura Tehnica* and would take control of events with a firm hand, relaxed and freshly shaven. He was no longer the "comrade Iliescu" who hid behind his desk during Gorbachev's visit. He had the excellent instincts and reflexes of a sly and experienced politician, and he staged a momentous conversion from an exotic fish to a great shark.

Actually, most Romanians knew it would happen like this. Ceausescu was aware of Iliescu's aims too, but he could not believe they would be the end of him. The Securitate knew as well but without Ceausescu's consent, it could not touch Iliescu, who was one of Moscow's men in Bucharest—which in the end would work to Kremlin's favor. Iliescu would largely spare the "organs" in the aftermath of the "coup-volution" (coup + revolution); only a handful of senior officers would be sent to prison and then released. To make things look more credible, he used the turmoil and confusion created by "terrorists" (whoever they were) to his advantage. The would-be terrorists were a smokescreen, but they would cause more than one thousand Romanians to die a stupid death. The terrorists were necessary to distract attention from the pro-Gorbachev group's coup. This group made the whole world believe that the pro-Ceausescu forces were fighting for their lives to defend the regime. "Look at these Romanian revolutionaries! How brave they are! See how they are dying for their freedom, fighting the Securitate "terrorists"? And you can watch the entire "revolution" on TV! This is the first revolution in human history broadcast live! How much bloodshed—what heroism!" I was proud, after so many years, that I was Romanian. My colleagues were talking about Romania with admiration. Their respect—and mine—didn't last too long, though.

Honestly speaking, nobody was trying to defend Ceausescu. Everybody hated him. Everything had been staged according to a plan, which the Securitate top dogs—such as General Vlad—were aware of. The naïve hoi polloi died "to defend" the revolution. The slyboots took advantage of their televised deaths and got what they wanted: the political and financial power.

Silviu Brucan was one of these men. I met him when he passed through Vienna in late 1988, after his visit to the United States and England. It's interesting that after he visited London, he went to Moscow, and then he flew to Vienna before returning to Bucharest by train.

In February of the same year, I interviewed him by phone, and he told me that he was under house arrest in Bucharest, after the violent repression of the workers' protests in Brasov in November 1987 that he supported. The protests, he said, foreshadowed the imminent collapse of Ceausescu. In March 1989 the AP bureau in Vienna received a copy of the "Letter of the Six," a left-wing critique of Ceausescu's policies written together with five other ex-Communist dignitaries posing as a group of inner-party dissidents.

What a character Brucan was! He joined the Party in his youth, and he did prosper after the Communist takeover following the war: he was a former ambassador to the United States, editor-in-chief of *Scanteia*, the Communist Party organ, and head of the state-owned TV. Though he disagreed with Ceausescu's policies after Nicolae became the new Party boss in the mid-1960s, he never gave up his communist beliefs and did not oppose communist ideology. For most of his political life, he was a Moscow agent. Placed under house arrest, the Soviet Embassy in Bucharest extended him protection, allowing him a relative degree of freedom. The *Conducator* did not dare to throw him in jail.

I went to the hotel where he was staying in Vienna, accompanied by Jolyon Naegele, the *Voice of America* bureau chief. Brucan gave the impression of being very well informed and connected to the officials in Washington and Moscow with whom he had discussed the situation in Romania. He said that Ceausescu's end was "near, even very near." He sounded convinced that this would happen in the next few days. Anyway, he needed both Moscow's support, which could provide the script of the "coup-volution" and Washington's backing, which offered the PR and advertising means through Radio Free Europe and *Voice of America*.

When I visited Romania in the spring of 1990, I learned that Brucan obtained his passport for his trips abroad with the approval of Iulian Vlad, the Securitate chief. At that time I had no idea what General Vlad had written in my dossier regarding my "disparagement" of Romania.

Vlad certainly knew of the pro-Gorbachev group's plans, but he closed his eyes, realizing that Ceausescu's days were numbered. He understood that Moscow wanted to get rid of him. However, he didn't join the revolutionaries until the last moment, not wishing to risk anything. He waited until Ceausescu fled by helicopter. That explains why the Securitate abandoned him so easily. The top generals knew what was about to happen, and Vlad ordered his troops to lie low and do nothing against the new authorities. If this is not treason, I don't know what is. What is the difference between Vlad and Pacepa? Pacepa betrayed Ceausescu for the Americans, and Vlad, who took an oath of allegiance to the regime like Pacepa, betrayed him for Iliescu and Co.

What General Vlad could not know was that after Ceausescu's removal, communism in Romania would expire too—the communism for which he had worked so zealously, with the firm belief that it was for the good of the Romanian people. It was the "ism" that meant everything to him and the others like him: a good life filled with all sorts of advantages for them. He couldn't know at that time that Gorbachev himself would be swept aside in less than two years by the hurricane that he had set in motion.

Arrested on December 31, a week after Ceausescu's execution, Vlad was sentenced to twenty-five years' imprisonment for his participation in the bloody suppression of the Timisoara revolt. The new authorities would release him after only four years. Later on, he would say that although he propped up the *Conducator* until the last moment, he was actually disenchanted by his personality cult. As a true communist and the Securitate top officer, he was not disillusioned by the crimes committed while he and others like him played the first fiddle. Why did he need such a long time to clarify his political views? He never regretted, at least publicly, being an abject *securist*. In public he liked to behave like a gentleman. What a smooth operator![27]

Unlike Vlad, General Alexie, head of the Counterintelligence directorate and Vlad's first deputy and confidante, was not even arrested. He was retired after less than a month. Knowledgeable Romanians said that Iliescu interceded on his behalf and allowed Alexie to go to France where he underwent heart surgery for a condition he had suffered from for some time.

After Ceausescu's flight I continued to listen to Radio Bucharest, the lone source of information about the events in the country. In the chaos after his escape, Western reporters still had a hard time getting to Bucharest.

The question on everybody's lips was what had happened to the "sinister couple" as Romanians sarcastically referred to Nicolae and his wife, Elena. There were tons of rumors. Listening to the radio on December 25, I heard a broadcaster's voice overflowing with joy as he proudly announced that the Ceausescus had been tried and sentenced to death. Their execution by an army firing squad had taken place the same day.

"Oh, what a wonderful news," the radio presenter kept repeating with happiness that was obviously not simulated. It was Christmas Day, and an old Romanian carol, which the regime had banned, could be heard to an unusual extent. For the twenty-three million Romanians, it was a double miracle: the news about the execution and the first free Christmas in forty years. The Antichrist, who had pulled down churches and imprisoned priests like Father Calciu, had been shot dead the day Jesus Christ was born. This had the symbolic significance of all Romanians returning to their traditional religious beliefs. Who would be the first to "reconnect" with the Creator and the saints, for whom he did not give a damn before?

---

27 In 2013, at the age of 82, Vlad was a counselor with the Romanian-Chinese Chamber of Commerce.

The new leader, Ion Iliescu. Under the old regime, Iliescu had criticized Romanians for going to church for weddings and for baptizing their babies, but now…he had the brilliant reflexes of a Romanian politician—as illustrated by the two world wars in which this country took part and, each time, it switched sides after the military winds changed direction. Or as history books put it succinctly, "Romania turned its weapons" abandoning the Axis powers after three years and joining practically overnight the victorious Allies. It was as simple as that.

I wrote a story about the Ceausescus' execution, adding that the event had been presented as a "divine gift." In the evening, I watched the clip from their trial. We couldn't pick up the Romanian TV from Vienna, so we watched Hungarian TV that showed it live for their Hungarian audience. They were as happy as their Romanian neighbors were.

There were reporters from many publications coming to our office, as they knew that I was able to provide translation from Romanian into English. Listening attentively, I could hear what the Ceausescus were saying to their accusers in the background. In the foreground, the TV translated simultaneously for the Hungarian viewers.

I could analyze the defenders' body language: unrepentant, sneering, confrontational, rejecting all accusations. But it was a strange trial—a farcical court case—and not only because it lasted only one hour. It was unreal to hear the defenders' counsel attacking the two more virulently than the prosecutor. The whole thing was a simple formality: a political masquerade where the sentence had been established before the trial. Ironically, it looked like one of the hundreds of Stalinist show trials of the 1950s.

The first of the accusations—genocide, in which sixty thousand Romanians died—triggered smiles of distrust from Western reporters. Genocide is the deliberate extermination of a large group of people, especially those belonging of a specific ethnic group, such as the Nazis' extermination of European Jews. This was not what Ceausescu did to Romanians. A few minutes after the death sentence was pronounced, the "sinister couple" was executed. It would have been better to let the mob deal with them at the Party headquarters. That's what a revolution is supposed to do.

A question troubled me, still. If "God has turned his face to Romania," as Dinescu said, how would Romanians respond? Would they flunk their reunion with history as they had so many times in their convoluted history?

\* \* \*

My arrival in Vienna along with my wife and our son in the fall of '87 was like my second time coming into this world. Vienna was something I could hardly fancy after Romania's empty shelves and dinginess. Food stores were brimming with delicacies. There were elegant streetcars, spotless subways, neat public parks where kids had their own playgrounds outfitted with colorful equipment and curving slides. And the city was so shiny at night! Think of all that "wastage" of electric energy. Where was Ceausescu to scold the Austrians for their extravagance?

I went to the *Wiener Staatsoper*, and I was amazed. I recalled the opera shows at home where, due to the lack of heat in the winter, the onlookers wore their heavy coats and the ballerinas had their trunks covered in flannel shirts...and I almost started laughing and crying at the same time.

Other things that shocked me were the sleek sedans, so quiet that I couldn't hear them coming until they were several feet away: sffsh...sffsh... and I was standing frozen in my boots when cars stopped abruptly to avoid hitting me. In Romania, you could hear the Dacias and the two-cylinder East German Trabants from three hundred feet away. They were as noisy as tractors.

Then there were the bananas. They were everywhere! I ate so many in the first several weeks that I had an indigestion. When you went to *Hauptbahnhof*, Vienna's main station, and saw the trains with tourists or émigrés coming from Eastern Europe, what was the first thing they were looking for? They were not looking for Swiss chocolate or American cigarettes—but the bananas. I saw people past middle age carrying two or three bunches of bananas victoriously and laughing like kids. Could this be the best proof that monkeys are our ancestors?

Talking about creatures, another thing that struck me were the special aisles filled with pets' food in the grocery stores. Much of the pet food looked so appealing that I thought it was for human consumption. Since they were eating so well, the dogs sometimes left a generous pile of excrement in the streets at night that was picked up by the city's sanitation workers in the morning. Until I became familiarized with the new situation, I thought the pile was of human nature. I asked a colleague why some people were relieving themselves in the street. He laughed heartily. "It's dog turd," he said.

"So bulky?" I asked incredulously. "In Romania the skinny dogs made a tiny, dry, and discolored piece of poop that the wind dispersed in less than two hours," I explained. I thought, "See the difference between the two political systems? Compare the capitalist dog excrement versus the communist shit. They beat us in this chapter, too. Dogs in the West were eating better than the working hoi polloi in the Soviet bloc.

The closer we got to late 1989, the more numerous the anti-communist demonstrations and protests that took place—reflecting the people's growing opposition to the one-party rule. The last domino piece, Romania, was the only place where the popular revolt occurred violently, with much bloodshed and chaos. My colleagues and I spent days and nights at the office, caught in the maelstrom of events, editing the stories sent by our correspondents in Prague, Budapest, Sofia, and Warsaw. It was a fascinating time to be in Vienna, the key outpost to the totalitarian East, and follow the falling of the dominoes, one after the other. The city was the center of the planet, facing the bubbling volcano that was erupting and tossing the communist parties to the Dumpster of history.

While I was editing those stories, my attention was focused on the situation at home. Unlike the other East European countries where we had local stringers, after my departure we didn't have anybody in Romania.

A story about the paying off of Romania's debt—which totaled $11 billion in 1981—got good play in the West. For the following eight years, while the debt got smaller, the lines at food stores got longer. Everything that the country produced went for export. The food shortages created a "language of misery" and an industry of gags: the chicken wings and necks were called "dishes"; the pig's feet were "adidas"; the pig's heads were cynically dubbed "computers," which could be with "radars" or "without radars," (i.e. ears). And the "patriots" were the pig's hooves, which never abandoned their country and didn't defect to the West, because they could not be exported.

> One after one communists are falling
> While on the street they're strolling.
> Holding their red Party card in their hand
> Starving—and shouting:
> "No food in the Promised Land?"

This was the *Conducator*'s "Golden Epoch." Unlike food and gasoline, the jokes were never in short supply. How can Romanians pay the foreign debt faster and without suffering? By auctioning the dictator's golden epoch. What's colder than the cold water? The hot water.[28]

In another story, I wrote about the political jokes in the Soviet bloc, the only industry that has always prospered under the communist regimes. In Prague, Frantisek Vencovsky, a senior economist in the state planning committee, used to tell Western reporters about the "miracles" of socialism: Everybody has a job, but nobody works. Nobody works, but all economic plans are fulfilled. All plans are fulfilled, but nothing is available. Nothing is available, and everything is perfect.

Here is another Czech wisecrack: What's socialism? The most difficult and painful road from capitalism to capitalism. And here's a Hungarian pun: What's the difference between communism and sex? Communism is all left, while sex is all right.

Romanians, who suffered the most because of shortages of all kinds, were so enthusiastic and zealous in producing political jokes that the

---

28 Google search:
Viorel Urma, "Romania Pays Off Its Debts But Problems Linger," April 23, 1989

Securitate had set up a special department charged with catching those who made fun of the *Conducator* and his family.

In the three years I spent in Vienna, I didn't write only political and economic stories but also sports and culture articles. Among others, I wrote a story from Salzburg about the celebrated music festival several months after Herbert von Karajan's death and the changes made to open the annual event to new forms of art and to musicians who were never invited there before.[29]

Two significant things happened to me in Vienna. One day my wallet disappeared while I was in the shower and alone in our apartment. Gone were my Romanian passport, the press badge issued to foreign reporters by the Austrian government, and the equivalent in schillings of $150. Nothing else. It will remain a mystery forever.

Secondly, around Christmas I got two late-night phone calls at home in which somebody speaking German threatened me with death. The death threats ceased in late December, after Marin Ceausescu, Nicolae's brother and head of Romania's Economic Agency in Vienna, was found with a rope around his neck in the basement of the embassy. In reality, he was the chief of the Romanian economic espionage in Western Europe.

I went to the Austrian police, and I demanded that they monitor my telephone traffic to see who was calling me. They refused, saying that several other people in Vienna had also received death threats, without offering me details. For a week after that, my wife, son and I lived in the apartment of a colleague whose parents were out of the country.

I didn't see any link between Ceausescu's brother and the phone calls that I received. I believed that it was more likely that they had an Arab connection. I had written two stories about "terrorists" in Romania, based on Radio Bucharest reports about the existence of Libyan and Palestinian special troops paid by Ceausescu to defend him. They were allegedly fighting the anti-regime revolutionaries.[30]

---

29 Viorel Urma, "Festival Reforms After von Karajan," August 31, 1989.
30 Viorel Urma, "Revolutionaries Find Scores of Arms-Laden Safe Houses and Tunnels," December 25, 1989.

"Come to defend the radio station; we are under attack by Arab troops. Come to defend our revolution," the radio announcers called repeatedly. In the background, I could hear the sound of gunshots and fighting. The calls sounded so dramatic and desperate that it was impossible to ignore them. According to the reports—some of them confirmed by the new authorities—planes from Libya and other Arab countries were flying to Bucharest to pick up the "Arab terrorists" and bring them home. My stories had been published across the Middle East and picked up by papers worldwide.

In Romania there were training camps for Yasser Arafat's Palestinian guerrillas and for Libyan and Syrian commandos led by Romanian military instructors. It was a very delicate subject. In an effort to quash those reports and save the Arabs from the fury of the masses, the Libyan ambassador felt that it was necessary to appear on Romanian TV and deny that Libyan citizens took part in the revolution.

Iliescu's first meeting with a foreign ambassador was with Libya's envoy. And the official Libyan radio, the Voice of the Greater Arab Homeland, reported a phone conversation between Gadhafi and Iliescu, in which the Romanian leader vehemently denied that Arab citizens were involved. He blamed "rumors spread by enemies in order to…influence our friendship with the Arabs."

In another twist, the fall of Communist governments across Eastern Europe would deprive the PLO and other Arab groups of weapons and training. Romania, Czechoslovakia, East Germany, and Poland provided varying degrees of material and political support to the PLO and other groups. The aid was halted or reduced. Romania, which from the late 1970s trained hundreds of PLO guerrillas at bases in the Black Sea port of Constanta and near Bucharest, announced shortly after Ceausescu's downfall that it abrogated the agreements that he concluded.[31]

Many things were said during those confusion-filled days…

---

31 Viorel Urma, "Upheavals in East Bloc Diminish Support for Arab Radicals," February 12, 1990.

Several months after the revolution, I went to Sibiu to report on the trial of Nicu, Ceausescu's youngest son, who was the head of the Communist Party in the Transylvanian city. He had been accused of genocide for the death of eighty-nine people in chaotic clashes between revolutionaries and the army on one hand and the Securitate forces on the other. Nicu, who was known as a playboy and a heavy drinker, was sentenced to twenty years in prison but was released after two years because he was suffering from terminal liver cancer.

After I arrived in New York in the fall of 1990, I traveled to Romania several times as a reporter to write about the abundance of stray dogs, corruption, poverty, and the frauds committed by the new politicians and the nouveaux riches. Those who had ties with the former Securitate before the revolution, like the controllers of Ceausescu's bank accounts both in the country and abroad, were prospering.[32] In Romania capitalism was doing good, fraud even better.

But back to my travels to Bucharest—I interviewed Adrian Nastase, who was a member of the leading Social Democratic Party, the successor of the Communist Party that rallied most of the former communists. We chatted about the first free elections in forty years and what was expected from them. He talked mechanically and without offering much substance. He was using the same wooden language as Iliescu, his boss, and regurgitating the same ideas.

I would interview him again when he would come to the United States as Romania's prime minister in November 2001. He stayed in a suite furnished with a bar at a luxury hotel in Manhattan, where I saw at least a dozen bottles of expensive drinks—none of them full.

I asked him about the booming corruption in the country—from small businesses to high-ranking politicians—and the numerous scandals that filled the pages of newspapers. Corruption was the main obstacle for Romania's entry into NATO, the Western military alliance.

---

32 Viorel Urma, "Romania Revisited: Barking Dogs, Corruption and Poverty," September 6, 1993.

"This is our number one objective. We have to attack corruption very seriously," he tried to convince me.[33]

"Could you name any lawbreakers who were caught and sentenced to jail?" Nastase could not give me any names. He was selling empty promises to his American hosts.

It was not possible that Romania, one of the most corrupt countries in Europe, had no prominent crooks caught and condemned if they were cracking down on corruption. According to the media, there were hundreds of economic offenders across the country. I was not talking about state bureaucrats who refused to help people with their daily problems, doctors who would not operate, or nurses who would not help patients without payment of *ciubuc* or *bacsis (baksheesh)*—both Turkish words that found a friendly ambience in Romania. I meant the fat sharks, with ties to the Securitate, the keeper of Ceausescu's fortune, who made millions overnight from the privatization of the former state enterprises, illicit real estate deals, and money laundering.

Nastase offered me a senseless explanation. "In America there was the same situation," he said. "Rockefeller made his first million from illegal transactions."

I thought, "Aha! If you are a thief, the first million obtained through unlawful means is OK. You are forgiven. If this happened in capitalist America, why wouldn't it be acceptable in capitalist Romania too?" It was preposterous for a prime minister to talk like this.

Ten years later, with Romania under special monitoring by the European Union due to pervasive high-level corruption, Nastase would join the growing numbers convicted felons, being charged with bribery and blackmail. When the police arrived at his home to arrest him, he shot himself in the throat with one of his collection guns in what appeared to be a cheap shot on his part to evade justice. It was like a soap opera. On that night, an ambulance removed him from his home with an expensive

---

33 Viorel Urma, "Romanian Premier: Fighting Corruption is a Political Objective," February 3, 2002.

Burberry scarf draped around his neck. After he received treatment in a hospital, he was moved to prison to serve his two-year term.

If it's true that John D. Rockefeller made his first million from illegal transactions with oil, he eventually became a great philanthropist. By all accounts, the former Romanian premier, whose moniker was Nastase *sapte case* (seven houses), made more than a million dollars in all sorts of shady deals. I am still wondering if he donated anything to charity.

The octopus of corruption, the unlawful enriching of many officials and politicians, as well as the poor administration of the economy would lead to the impoverishment of the population. The gangrene of fraud would directly affect the Romanians' standard of living, and many young adults would leave the country to look for a job in the West. The worst thing that can happen is when the youth lose their hopes for a better future.

Yes, God may have turned his face toward Romanians, but they failed to answer in kind. He gave them a chance, and they largely squandered it.

# 12

*What a beautiful country! It has mountains, lakes, forests,*
*woods, rivers... Too bad it is inhabited by corrupt politicians and*
*inept public officials.*

—MODERN ROMANIAN ADAGE

Bucharest
Spring 2014

I am vacationing in Romania, and I am curious to read my secret police
dossier and see how the country has progressed since the 2008 global
recession. Romanians celebrate two important events this year: it's been
twenty-five years since the revolution and ten years since their admission
to the NATO military alliance. It is May, and the elections to the European
Parliament in the EU member countries, including Romania, are on everybody's political agenda.

At the Otopeni International Airport, I am impressed by the cleanli-
ness and the civility I'm greeted with at the entrance gate to the country.[34]
Passport formalities go fast and smoothly. The baggage carousel is quick,
and I pick up my suitcase and go out to the parking lot. There has been a
lot of rain, and the air is clean and refreshing. The high levels of dust and
grit, so characteristic of this city on a plain, are not present today. The hot
and dusty months are July and August.

---

34 The new formal moniker is Henri Coanda International Airport, named after the scientist referred to in Chapter 3. The change was thought necessary after some officials
realized, after many years, that Otopeni—the name of the old town near the airport—was
drawing smiles from some foreign visitors. In Italian, *otto peni* means "eight penises."

In the following days, after tours of the downtown area and several districts, I'll be pleasantly surprised by the upgraded look of the capital—in particular the Historical Center, the four-hundred-year-old district of artisans and merchants that emerged around the Princely Court in the sixteenth century. The old town was overhauled in recent years and turned into a trendy entertainment district and is now a favorite hangout for locals and foreign visitors. The daunting buildings in French baroque style, the old churches—gems of architecture—the sidewalk terraces and cafés, and the reverie feel make this a tantalizing place in the city.

I notice that there are fewer stray dogs, the decrepit facades of some of the communist-era, drab apartment blocks have been revamped, and the car traffic—usually a bit on the nightmarish side—is more disciplined. In another sign of progress, Bucharestians seem to have stopped unloading their pockets of scraps of paper in the middle of the street. Some are even cleaning after their pets! This never happened before. This must the positive influence of the West, as Romanians can now travel freely and see how others are behaving in public.

What has not changed—and actually seems to have gotten worse—are the adjectives and invectives the politicians use. They are inspired by the political commentators, who contribute in their turn to the escalation of the toxicity level of the political discourse. In Romania, if you don't know how to bad-mouth your opponents, you don't stand a chance in politics. It has always been like this, except for the communist period when the obscenities were channeled by the many to the Great Leader and the Beloved Party—a single party and a single honcho that attracted all the dirty words like a magnet. It was more simple and efficient, and the people felt united in their loathing, which gave them more relief.

After the totalitarian shackles fell, Romania is now a free country—honeycombed with corruption. Many unjust things happen, but they are often of little international significance. It's easy to be covered by the Western media, which usually don't have an ear for the daily gossip and rumormonger. They know that people of Latin volatility talk much—especially in TV talk shows and other public debates—and do little.

What is relevant—such as the country's participation in NATO and its role on the eastern flank of the military alliance, the economic crisis, the

IMF talks, the presidential elections, and the struggle against corruption—is reported in a maximum of five hundred words.

Sometimes I think I would like to again work as a correspondent here. But I better not. Before, it was challenging to find out what was going on and to get details. Everything was censored, and it was risky to investigate by yourself. Now the dirty linen is washed in public, on TV, or on the internet, and all the details are readily available…but what's their weight? The politicians who consume each other?

Reading the press releases from the *Directia Nationala Anticoruptie* (DNA), the anticorruption watchdog tasked with preventing, investigating, and prosecuting corruption-related offences—such as bribery, graft, and embezzlement—one concludes that the political class is so determined to enrich itself that those in it utterly ignore all the consequences. "Let's stuff our pockets first and go to jail later," they probably say.

Nine former ministers, including a member of the European Parliament, were incriminated in a huge bribery and money-laundering scandal involving distributors selling Microsoft products in the country. According to the DNA, the ministers backed an illegal contract with Fujitsu Siemens Computers to lease Microsoft licenses at inflated prices, allowing some of them to embezzle a huge discount that Microsoft gave to the Romanian government. The DNA says that of the $54 million paid by the government under the contract, $20 million ended up in the pockets of state officials. The scandal, dubbed in the media as Romania's "Microsoftgate," allowed the state to circumvent public auctions of IT services.

A plagiarism scandal has rocked the office of Prime Minister Victor Ponta, a former Adrian Nastase protégé, who stands accused of plagiarizing more than half of his 2004 doctoral thesis. Academic plagiarism is commonplace in the country. Ponta's education minister was accused of copying material in a book that he wrote about Romania. The second education minister also resigned under similar circumstances. According to media reports, teachers are said to take bribes regularly, and even degrees can be bought.

In another infamous case, a former Romanian minister of youth and sport, and ex-member of the European Parliament, was sentenced to five years' imprisonment for abuse of office and embezzlement. The anti-corruption prosecutors said she diverted 640,000 euros to two start-up companies for organizing the annual Youth Day celebrations—much above the required amount. The two companies were newly established and had joint headquarters in an apartment; they had the same shareholders.

The parliament, referred to sarcastically in the media as "Romania's penal parliament," is arguably the most corrupt body of politicians in Europe, with at least fifty senators and deputies charged with committing offenses that are punishable by law.

It goes on and on and on.

In this respect, the country has not changed much in 150 years. There is a story of how Carol I lost his wallet during a banquet given for him in 1866 when he arrived in Bucharest as a young German prince to take over the throne. Ion Bratianu, a prominent politician and future prime minister, promptly called for attention and announced:

"Someone present reports that his wallet has been taken. The candles will be extinguished for three minutes. By the time they are relighted, I expect the missing wallet to be on the silver platter in the center of the table."

When the candles were relighted, the silver platter was also gone.

(Another version is that there were six wallets in the center of the table when the lights came on).

Watching the TV roundtable debates is a rewarding experience. Before starting to contradict each other in cross talk, the commentators and analysts proudly place their smartphones on the table in front of them while heatedly discussing political issues, the way the Wild West outlaws did when they went to the saloon and dropped their guns on the counter. This is the Wild East after all, where cellphones and invectives have replaced guns and bullets. Do they have to check their phones for messages from their managers? "Say this, don't say that…" I ask myself if this is a sign of disrespect toward viewers. You don't see this in the United States, where excessive good manners are seldom the rule.

\* \* \*

One day I was walking in the A. I. Cuza Park in Bucharest's Third District when I saw a group of youngsters dressed in red shirts and pants who were distributing leaflets that said, "We're proud to be Romanian! Vote PSD." On the other side was a photo of Ponta, Romania's copy-paste prime minister, accompanied by the text, "We send to Brussels people who are proud to be Romanians [and who] will defend Romania!" At the bottom, there was this appeal: "Strong Romania in Europe!" Being curious, I accepted the leaflet that was handed to me, and with it I got a white cigarette lighter that urged me to "Vote PSD" (Social Democratic Party). While I was reading the leaflet, one of the purveyors of trinkets gave me another lighter, as a bonus probably. Not everybody accepted the leaflets. Some park visitors cursed the center-left successor of the Communist Party but accepted the lighter nevertheless.

"You know," I said to myself, "this is a useful thing. It comes in handy. I came from the United States without a lighter, and although I am an occasional smoker, it's good to have one." The next day, when I was relaxing in the same park—which looked terrific with its sea of fresh flowers, power-operated artesian wells, manicured lawns, and a lake crisscrossed by rowboats—I got a yellow lighter from another "political group" of young people. This lighter urged me to vote PNL (National Liberal Party). "I'll take it, thanks." I was in a euphoric mood. If I kept walking in Bucharest, I would be able to obtain more lighters than I had ever had. Nobody hands you lighters, ball pens, key chains, calendars, refrigerator magnets, and other cheap crap before elections in the United States. Before presidential elections in Romania, they even hand out bags of white flour, sugar, cornmeal, and bottles of cooking oil to the needy Romanians to encourage them to vote "correctly." If you get such things why refuse them? You throw away the goddamn leaflet and keep the lighter or the ball pen. The text—"We're proud we are Romanians"—looked tolerably idiotic to me. Only the governing PSD was "proud" of that? In the United States, they would say "We're proud [all of us] to be American," or they'd find another catchphrase.

My wife and I went to vote for the country's delegates to the European Parliament, but we came across a little problem. Not having to show a regular ID with permanent residency in Romania, we showed them our

Romanian passports that said we are residing in the United States. That did not impress an official from the supervising commission who said that the document we showed is valid for traveling but not for voting purposes. "Look," I explained, "we have dual citizenship. We're on vacation here. Do you want us to vote in Romania on the basis of our US passports?" My mocking question irked him, but I didn't give in. "I am eligible to vote at the Romanian Consulate in New York when there are national elections in Romania, but we can't do this in the country where we were born? How's that?"

I know what he was thinking. Most Romanians living abroad usually don't vote the socialist PSD, preferring instead the center-right parties. Knowing that we came from the United States, he assumed this would be our case and decided, therefore, that it was better not to allow us to cast our votes at all. I guessed that he represented the PSD there—the "white lighter" party—and not the "yellow lighter" of the main opposition party. Luckily for us, the head of the voting commission checked the law and concluded that we were eligible to vote, and our passports issued by the Romanian authorities were a valid ID.[35]

In the voting booth, after reading the list of the dozen or so parties, I chose to cast my vote for the center-right People's Movement,[36] the "blue jeans party" which represented Romania's youth. I was wearing a pair of jeans too, although I was no longer young. I liked one of the ideas of their political platform: "We strengthen our partnership with the USA…and we bring Moldova to Europe." As their motto said, "The Movement makes the improvement." "So be it! Good luck, guys," I said to myself, and I rubber stamped the PMP logo as was required. They hadn't given me a lighter or a key chain during my strolls through Bucharest. They didn't buy me.

---

35 Bureaucratic procedures and insufficient voting booths led to thousands of Romanians living abroad not being able to vote in the presidential elections in November. Many saw this as a strategy of the governing socialists to exclude voters who would otherwise cast their vote for the center-right parties—which was true, as most of the Romanians in diaspora voted not for Victor Ponta but for Klaus Iohannis who was elected president.

36 Elena Udrea, former president of PMP and an influential politician, would later be incriminated in the Microsoft scandal on counts of influence peddling, money laundering, and receipt of 500,000 euros.

After exercising my constitutional right as a citizen, I watched the TV political debates and comments after the European Parliament elections. There was huge drama: the leadership of the center-right PNL—which came in second—submitted their resignations *en bloc*, including president Crin Antonescu and vice president Klaus Iohannis (who would become Romania's president in November); the leaders of the other center-right party, PDL—which got the third spot—were "humbled in the dust, with long faces;" PMP, at the bottom but still in jeans, "seemed to rejoice over the results, though they were expecting more." On the other hand, the leaders of the center-left PSD—which came out as winners and would send more delegates than the other parties to Brussels—were "happy though they had hoped to score a more convincing victory."

"The elections are over; the war continues," flashed a TV breaking-news story. Everybody knows this. The clashes won't stop here. Romanians, like Greeks, are pathologically obsessed by politics. They are temperamentally unsuited for the art of statecraft. Now they are splitting hairs and sharpening the long knives, figuratively. There is much ado about nothing, since nothing is going to change.

The commentators talk ad nauseam about "coagulation"—an unfortunate word. They talk of "the coagulation of the center-right forces" in their battle against the center-left PSD. According to moderator Madalina Puscalau, "This appears to be an impossible mission" because the opposition has been too divided and unable to speak with just one voice. I wish they could find another word. In the United States, only doctors know what coagulation means.

I watch Radu Banciu, a controversial commentator, whose show, "Banciu's World," is a lively critique of the political menagerie and circus in Romania, where elections or referendums are mudslinging spectacles and opportunities for politicians to settle old scores publicly.

Banciu doesn't spare anybody. He paints with a broad brush and tells things with brutality and cynicism. In societies in which political correctness has been elevated to state policy, few have the nerve to call things by name. Banciu would be fired if his show were in the United States. He would be fined and sued for racism, misogyny, calumny, defamation, and who knows what else. It would be good to have an American Banciu; only the United States is less cynical than Europe and more hypocritical. (With PC running rampant, I was not surprised to see on my daily commute to New York on all NJ Transit buses a notice telling riders that the front seats are reserved for "pregnant people" and other situations. Pregnant people? Men and women? Can Vladimir Putin get pregnant? Or Barak Obama? If not, you guys are not allowed to take those seats, even if you are presidents)

"Who can you vote for? Politicians are no role models. They are too hungry for power. By voting you feed a bunch of rascals," Banciu says. On the other hand, "To be a good politician these days, you must know how to disgrace and lower yourself to the imbecility of those who cast their votes for you," he adds. "Politics is a whore of circumstances…The political class is losing ground," he concludes.

What he says has universal validity. Everywhere you look, in Europe or in the United States, there are fewer and fewer competent and intrepid statespersons. In Europe, apart from Angela Merkel (as of this writing), there are no accomplished politicians. (A year later, she'll be castigated by some for opening the borders of Germany, and of Europe, in general, to millions of refugees from the Middle East). The overpaid European Union bureaucrats in Brussels with their tales about Europe's "new political architecture" and open borders seem to live in a fantasy world.

In the United States, no president has achieved anything notable since Reagan, Bush Sr., and Clinton. Bush Jr. messed up big time in Iraq and indirectly brought the US economy to its knees, and Obama, after the choruses of praise six years ago, has become President Pinocchio on some social media. In cyberspace he is called "Trojan horse politician, fool, divider, narcissistic moron, traitor," and "enemy of our great nation." Mark Levin, a lawyer and author, said in a TV interview that Obama is an "incompetent and unfocused" president and that "everything he touches turns to crap." Lech Walesa said that by failing to lead, the Obama administration has been a dangerous disappointment.

Bush Jr. was labeled with such epithets as "terrorist pig, dog, Dumbo, and Bushilter," being likened to Adolf Hitler in some internet postings. Trolls are turning the web into a cesspool of verbal agression and violence.

Europe is not doing any better. Karl Lagerfeld, the fashion creator for Chanel, called President Francois Hollande "imbecile" because he hiked taxes for the rich. According to Italian newspapers, the phallic Prime Minister Silvio Berlusconi—alias Mr. Bunga Bunga for his lewd sex scandals—was once overheard referring to Merkel as a *culone inchiavabile* (unscrewable fat ass), while British Premier David Cameron has been gratified in online communities with such sobriquets as "bastard" and "glistening, meat-faced dolt." Putin, the steely faced son of the KBG, is "Khuilo" (from the Russian word for "*khui*"—penis). Bush Jr.'s nicknames for the vertically challenged Putin are "Pootie-Poot" and "Ostrich Legs."

In Romania, the war of invectives is red hot, resembling a boxing bout where the adversaries punch each other incessantly:

To Banciu, ex-President Iliescu is a "mongrel" of Romanian politics.

To Iliescu, Antonescu, the leader of the main opposition party, is a "lick-spittle, a man devoid of substance."

To Antonescu, Prime Minister Victor Ponta "is stricken with anti-democratic dementia."

To Tariceanu, a Liberal leader, Antonescu is an "unstable traitor."

To Antonescu, Tariceanu is "politically illiterate."

This is democracy in the twenty-first century. The more politicians' promises turn to "crap," the higher the people's wave of resentment and distrust.

According to cynics, politicians tell the truth in only one situation: when they call each other liars. How are the Western democracies, buffeted by all sorts of crises, going to survive if they are led by inept politicians, without vision and mettle?

Ninety years ago, H. L. Mencken saw how things would evolve in the future.

"Democracy is a pathetic belief in the collective wisdom of individual ignorance," he said.

Totalitarian regimes—like Iran and North Korea, where the "collective wisdom" is concentrated in the hands of one man, the Supreme Leader or the Dear Leader, who decides for everybody—can breathe easy. They don't lose sleep over free elections and political correctness. That's a huge advantage for them.

I wish the West had a leader. No dear, no supreme; just a leader with brains and balls.

* * *

My efforts to see my Securitate dossier lasted nine years. I petitioned the National Council for the Study of the Securitate Archives. I made phone calls from New York, and each time I talked to them, I was told to wait: "Your request is in our attention." Well, thank you.

I had almost lost hope when I got an e-mail from Virgiliu Tarau, the Council's vice president, in January 2014 informing me that "following investigations in our archives…we identified the microfilm of a file put together by the former Securitate." He said the microfilm had 108 cadres, some of them "partial legible." I thanked him, but I said that I was still waiting to see my full dossier for which I had petitioned in 2005. Shortly afterward they informed me that they had located it in their archives and invited me to come any time to see it.

* * *

Before seeing my Securitate dossier, in hopes of fully documenting my days as an AP reporter in Ceausescu's Romania, I wanted to see my file with the passports department—which before the communism's demise was run by the police, as it is still today. I went there a month before Romania's entry into the European Union in 2007. However, my experience with the police bureaucrats contrasted sharply with the encounter at the Council, where the officials were helpful and welcomed my request for photocopying thirty-two pages from my dossier for my possession.

Police Col. Goga Savu showed me into the spare, dimly lit room where a female officer with an inquisitive expression awaited us. My heart quickened as I saw what lay on a table in front of her: a thick folder labeled File B. 193.132.

"Have a seat, and take your time. It doesn't start chronologically, so if you're looking for older papers and documents, they are at the end," said Savu, chief of the General Evidence Department and Archive of the General Directorate of Passports. (They love long, tortuous titles in Romania).

Savu made it clear that this was not my Securitate dossier. Still, these pages were part of my life. "This is your passport dossier," he explained, and the female officer, who never introduced herself, nodded approvingly.

"I know," I said. "They're still looking for my secret police file. How many pages does this file have?"

"About two hundred. Any documents concerning your wife have been removed. We took them out before you came—and your son's too," Savu said, trying to sound jovial. "They have their own files, but the law doesn't permit you to see them."

"My son was only seven years old when we left Romania for good in 1987," I said. "I didn't know that he had a file."

"Good grief," I thought, "a two-hundred-page passport file for somebody who was allowed to travel abroad just once as an AP reporter." I quickly saw, however, that the file went beyond passport issues. One police report was clearly based on an observation from prying, envious neighbors. They noted that I must work for some foreign agency since the car I drove home—our humble office Skoda—had a license plate starting with 12-B, a combo reserved for foreign-owned vehicles.

Thumbing through the file, I saw a letter from an AP executive to Romania's Foreign Ministry asking why my application for a passport to cover the 1984 Los Angeles Olympics had been turned down. Another passport request—and refusal—came when I was invited to visit the AP headquarters in New York in the early 1980s. At the bottom of my application, in big, red letters was this notation: *Attention! Brother fled to USA.*

Obviously, I was a marked man.

But I was elated just to see the bureaucratic, ungrammatical Romanian and mangled facts in my passport dossier. It said I had relatives abroad besides my defector brother—false—and that I locked up my house's courtyard to keep out "unauthorized persons"—again false.

One entry written by a semiliterate communist-era cop translated this way: "In our evidence, he doesn't figure as a suspicious person…[but] I propose that we manifest prudence" in deciding whether he can travel to the West.

A letter dated June 3, 1987, records approval for my "definitive departure" from Romania. The government had suddenly seen the wisdom in getting rid of me, after ignoring requests from AP management and US diplomats to let me continue as a correspondent. Attached was my written pledge not to "damage under any circumstances the interests of the Romanian state... and its prestige" after I left the country. "What prestige?" I wondered. What a bunch of kooks!

As I read on, I started laughing. I was in a buoyant mood. But my humor dried up when I asked if I could photocopy a few pages from the file to show my family.

"Our copier is not in good shape," Police Col. Savu responded, showing a blackened page in an effort to dissuade me.

I insisted, however, and Savu instructed me to write a letter to his superiors specifying the pages I wanted. Two days later, he called to say I could pick up my four pages by presenting a bank receipt showing that I'd paid the equivalent of sixty-five cents for the cost of the copies.

The problem was that Romanian bureaucracy didn't collapse along with communism. No bank would accept my payment of this "consular tax" because I wasn't a Bucharest resident. I pleaded with a clerk at the passport office to accept direct payment, but she refused. "We know it's a problem sometimes, but...you can't pay here," she said firmly.

"You don't accept my payment of sixty-five cents when the corrupt politicians accept millions of dollars in bribes and kickbacks?" I thought. "Of course, you could give me the four pages free. What's sixty-five cents for the state's coffers, when state officials embezzle hundreds of millions? You still want to squeeze me seventeen years after the revolution, I see. You guys have a long way to go to join the ranks of honorable people, but don't count on me to join you where you are. I never was like you, and I will never be."

I was sixty-five cents away from owning something precious from my past, and I was furious. Slamming the door behind me, I let off a stream of Romanian expletives.

"Screw you!" I hollered, and then I started laughing. "I am the winner of this game! And you—a bunch of incompetent bureaucrats together with your screwed up copier."

# 13

*Russia is a "gas station" masquerading as a country. In fact,*
*Russia is a gas station run by a Mafioso.*

—Sen. John McCain

New York
Spring 2014

Elite Russian troops, in unmarked, green army uniforms, conquered Crimea in one day without firing a single shot. The little green men, equipped with state-of-the-art Russian weaponry and communication gear, showed an unusual professionalism for the Russian army.

It happened after Ukraine's former president and Moscow's man in Kiev, Victor Yanukovich, fled to Russia after the protests of hundreds of thousands of Ukrainians who wanted their country to develop closer ties with the West. For the ex-KGB agent Vladimir Putin, this represented an affront that could not be left unpunished. Mother Russia, like any true mother, could not abandon its disobedient baby, Ukraine. Communist dad Leonid Brezhnev had shown the same maternal (or paternal) love for Czechoslovakia in 1968. That's how responsible parents behave.

In Crimea the bulk of the population is made up of ethnic Russians, and they felt "threatened" by the new Ukrainian authorities who declared their diminished attachment to Russia's maternal feelings.

For the West the problem was not only how to punish daddy-in-chief Putin but also to find out what else he planned. Did he intend to annex the eastern part of Ukraine, which meant the de facto division of the country of forty-six million? Did he want to annex Trans-Dniester, the narrow strip of land sandwiched between Moldova and Ukraine? Or was he planning the return of Moldova and the Baltic sisters to Moscow's kindergarten? Did "Superputin," the martial arts enthusiast, plan to remake the lost empire? If so, was Crimea the first step in that process? He had already reinstated the former national anthem that was written during Stalin's time, changing only the words...

At the global headquarters of the Associated Press in New York, breaking news and stories from Ukraine, Russia, and from all over the world are popping up minute by minute. "Putin asserts right to use force," one headline says. "Pro-Russian gunmen made inroads in eastern Ukraine; Combat vehicles in east Ukraine fly Russian flag," says another. "NATO ups military presence amid Russian threat;" and there were many others like these.

At my desk, I continue to select and edit US financial and business stories for AP's overseas clients, but I sneak a peek at a small TV when CNN reporters from Kiev are broadcasting live. Somebody who was born in and lived for forty years in Romania cannot disconnect himself from that geographical area and break with the history of Eastern Europe, under any circumstances. I know more European history and geography than my colleagues do—history as it happened in real life, not history from books. I am the only one who was born and educated in that part of the world. I don't confuse Bucharest with Budapest, and Albania with Albany, the capital of New York. And I know that there is a difference between Balkans and Baltics, as there is between Moldova and Maldive (Islands).

Since I arrived in New York in the fall of 1990, I worked on AP's International Desk editing world copy and writing stories about life in the United States, before becoming a financial editor. I also covered two World Cup soccer competitions.

Here come several AP headlines from Romania: "US sending additional Marines to Romania" and "President says Russia may push down to Romania," in which Traian Basescu claims that Moscow might have territorial ambitions in Moldova and southern Ukraine "from Odessa to the Danube mouth and the Chilia arm," that used to be the border with the Soviet Union. (Remember how Moscow used to "steal" two square kilometers of new territory every year from the alluvium and feces, which the river collected from the old continent? Now the left bank of the Chilia arm—the Danube's longest and most vigorous, with two secondary internal deltas and one micro delta under formation—is in Ukraine. At least in this case, Ukraine is a winner by getting a little bigger each year.)

I see the headline of another story from the military base at Campia Turzii in Transylvania: "450 US, Romanian troops in joint military games." Man, what a show! It took quite a long time for the Americans to come to Romania, and the Romanians wanted them in their country badly after World War II. And here they are now to defend us against the former Big Brother. I thought, "You guys are seventy years late, but thank you for your consideration anyway."

I recall how we were taught to defend the "revolutionary conquests" of the working class and fight against the imperialist NATO aggressor led by the United States during the six months of military training after college graduation. Instead of Nike Ajax and Nike Hercules ground-to-air missiles, that our officers seemed so concerned with, Romania was invaded and conquered peacefully by Nike shoes capitalism! The countries flip-flopped from enemies to best friends! How the wheel of history turns!

While the United States and the West ponder how to respond to Moscow's aggression and what measures to take to prevent other actions, it becomes evident that the only viable response should be financial and economic—not military, because nobody wants to start an open war with Putin. A political war? Fine. But how exactly will it be implemented?

Being a financial editor, I have an idea: the Soviet Union lost the Cold War mostly for economic reasons. Reagan fooled them with the Star Wars program, forcing the Russians to spend billions on costly military technology. Instead of Star Wars, what's needed now is Pipeline Wars so that Western Europe becomes less dependent on Russian natural gas and oil. That will hit the Russians at their point of vulnerability and bankrupt their economy, as energy exports make up more than half of federal budget revenues. Russia is a huge gas station where vodka is served cheaply, and both gas and vodka are flowing plentifully.

I ask Steve Hurst, the former CNN bureau chief in Moscow in the '90s, to write a story on this topic. Steve, who currently works in the AP bureau in Washington, says it's a good idea. The idea may be good, but its application is going to take some time because there is no adequate infrastructure in place, although the United States has become the world's biggest producer of energy. We are not talking about laying subsea pipelines from the United States or Canada to Europe, but exporting liquefied natural gas by ship over the Atlantic. That will take three or four years. Until then, one way Europe can become less dependent on Russian exports of oil and gas is to use the new technology of extracting hydrocarbons from oil shale. Many Europeans oppose this. Europe is not the United States, with its vast, unpopulated spaces and sizeable shale deposits. Another way would be to build liquefied gas plants and terminals on the continent and lay new pipelines bypassing Russia.

Therefore, instead of a military war, we get a war of words. President Obama is a master in drawing red lines and warning that if you cross them, there will be "costs." What kind of "costs" did Russia pay for receiving Edward Snowden with open arms? US prosecutors charged him with theft of government property and willful communication of classified intelligence, but Snowden is doing fine, enjoying Putin's protection.

Obama warned Iran several times not to operate clandestine nuclear facilities, he warned Syria several times not to use chemical weapons against its people during the civil war, and now he threatens Putin with economic and financial sanctions that will cripple the Russian economy.

John Kerry, bombastically and self-importantly, starts babbling strange combinations of words and threats without any practical meaning. If Moscow annexes Crimea, he declares that "it will face a very serious series of steps" from the United States and European Union. Serious series of steps? My God, what a talented windbag.[37]

---

37 Kerry once said, "The President is desirous of trying to see how we can make our efforts in order to find a way to facilitate." (Remarks at NATO meeting on the Ukrainian crisis, April 1, 2014). What he meant was, "The President wants to help."

While a Snowden solution seems distant, the West announces financial sanctions that would eventually lead to the collapse of the ruble and the Moscow stock market, the flight of capital investment, and the kickoff of running inflation and economic recession.

Where are the golden times for Russia when communism was in full bloom? Ah, those years were unbelievable. In East Berlin in 1953, Budapest in 1956, and in Prague in 1968, it was so easy to send Soviet tanks for a pleasure ride on European roads. There was no MOEX (Moscow Exchange) at that time for transactions with stocks and bonds. The ruble was not convertible, and nothing was in danger of falling. The state was almighty, and nobody dared to move a finger, from Moscow to East Berlin. Well, actually, somebody did fall at that time: Brezhnev, from his bed when he got drunk.

Capitalist Russia is suffering now.

CNN shows Obama's press conference at NATO headquarters in Brussels after a meeting of foreign ministers of the member countries. He looks tired and bored, and he has lost weight since he was reelected president two years ago.

When former Senator Obama addressed adoring crowds in Berlin in 2008, he promised to "remake the world once again." These days he tries to reassure nations that his administration is not spying and listening in to Angela Merkel's and other European leaders' phone calls. Where is the gifted orator full of verve and energy, promising hope and change to 300 million Americans? Where is the mortal who addressed the crowds like a god? Exuding an air of a superior creature chosen by a special destiny, the new Messiah looked down at the crowds who watched him fascinated, charmed by his logorrhea: big words and even bigger promises mixed up with lies, so necessary when political interests demanded. Now he doesn't talk about "hope" and "change," his version of Gorbachev's "glasnost" and "perestroika." "Yes, we can!" was deliberately forgotten. What can we do?

Since he became president, the US economy has limped along. It is the weakest economic recovery since World War II. There are seventeen million jobless Americans, fifty million on food stamps, and the national debt is $17.5 trillion—$7 trillion more than when he took over. (By the end of Obama's second term, the debt would hit a whopping $20 trillion). Those who find work are making less money than before, and middle class incomes are decreasing. This isn't the fundamental change he talked about.

Obama promised "transparency" in Washington. Not only did that not happen, but also the secret mania within his administration deepened. The United States' largest news organizations lodged a complaint against the White House for imposing unprecedented limitations on photojournalists covering the president and harming the public's ability to monitor its own government.

In an opinion piece published in the *New York Times* headlined "Obama's Orwellian Image Control," AP's director of photography, Santiago Lyon, said the restrictions on press photographers covering the president were "draconian." He called official photo releases "propaganda."

In another instance, the Justice Department secretly seized the telephone records of about one hundred AP reporters in an effort to track down the source who disclosed an alleged Yemen terrorist plot story. AP described it as a "massive and unprecedented intrusion" into news-gathering operations.

When was the last time that an American president sought to control the independent media? Is this worse than Nixon? The current attitude seems to be: Yes, we can!

A report on press freedom in the United States published by the Committee to Protect Journalists, which usually advocates for press freedoms overseas, blamed Obama for ushering in a paralyzing climate of fear for both reporters and their government sources.

"The Obama Administration and the Press: Leak Investigations and Surveillance in Post—9/11 America" was written by Leonard Downie Jr., former executive editor of the *Washington Post*. He spoke with dozens of journalists who told him officials are "reluctant to discuss even unclassified information [...] because they fear that leak investigations and government surveillance make it more difficult for reporters to protect them as sources." In truth, the Obama administration has used the Espionage Act to go after whistle-blowers who leaked to journalists more than all previous administrations combined.

Even the executive editor of the *New York Times*, a newspaper that usually sings Obama's praises, had something to criticize.

"I would say it is the most secretive White House that I have ever been involved in covering…," Jill Abramson told Al Jazeera America in an interview. (Several months later, the paper set her free).

James Risen, a veteran *New York Times* reporter, said that the Obama administration is "the greatest enemy of press freedom that we have encountered in at least a generation." The administration wants to "narrow the field of national security reporting."

Does Obama have anything to hide? To cover up? He doesn't react like a Western leader. Immune to criticism and above it, his reflexes are more like those of an apparatchik from the former Soviet bloc. His political instincts and fondness for public adulation are also the same. The "Fountain of Wisdom." The "Trusted Commander in Chief." He would definitely like to regulate Fox News, known for its tough coverage of his policies… only that this is America, not Mao's China!

Overseas, the president has been bedraggled by foreign-policy controversies, including Egypt, where he bet on Muslim Brotherhood's Mohamed Morsi, and lost, and Syria, where he didn't intervene. In Libya, where he got involved, the despot that was ousted, Gadhafi, was better than those attempting to take his place. Iraq seems paralyzed by the ISIS blitzkrieg, the fanatical jihadist group that aims at establishing an Islamic state and is killing Christians and Shia Muslims whenever possible. In Afghanistan, after the US troops' withdrawal, Taliban will get the upper hand, no doubt.

A specter is haunting the world, and this time it is not the specter of communism but of Islamic extremism, which threatens everybody. Left unchecked, extremists will seek to extend their influence through acts of terrorism or even open war.

Carried away by a wave of juvenile optimism, which replaced the pragmatism required for a successful foreign policy, Obama thought that if he opened talks or had direct contacts with the United States' enemies, he—the modern Son of Man—could settle all problems. All could be accomplished through "conversations" and good intentions.

Now the issue is Ukraine. It's too much for Obama to handle, domestically and externally. He would prefer to play golf in Hawaii. Let others fix the problems, some of which he inherited from his predecessor.

The United States looks tired and apathetic after wars in Afghanistan and Iraq. After all, many are asking aloud, why should we be the world's policeman? We are fed up with fighting, and if the United States is not directly attacked, why bother? Let all take care of themselves.

Well, the results tell the whole story. If the United States is not leading, those who were waiting for the right moment to promote their interests fill the power vacuum. You don't have to go to Harvard Law School to know that.

Examples of this principle include Islamic terrorists or Putin's Russia. "The Beast from the East" thinks that now is the right moment for Moscow to nurture its expansionist policies. Like in a chess game, the moves were calculated in advance. Crimea is already lost to Ukraine. The question is how the West will react to Moscow's future movements.

As Henry Kissinger summed up part of the past six years, "Ukraine has lost Crimea; Russia has lost Ukraine; the U.S. has lost Russia; and the world has lost stability."

So, what's better: a strong United States that can make errors of judgment in its foreign policy but is feared and respected or a leader like Putin who wants to dominate others? A superpower that leads actively and democratically or an autocracy like Russia that treads on other people's rights?

\* \* \*

Today I plan to eat out. It has been a snowy winter and a cold spring, and I need to move my legs, not only my fingers on the computer's keyboard. Our lunch break is only half an hour, so I have to move fast.

Just across the street from Penn Station, there are good eats to be found. I enter an Italian deli, and I decide to order a roast-beef sandwich. A dozen people wait in line, and two college-age males with backpacks are in line in front of me having an animated discussion. Both are wearing Red Sox sweatshirts, and I conclude that they came by train from Boston during the spring break. One of them asks me for a quarter, and after I gave it to him, I ask a question in turn: "You must be college students on vacation. What do you think about Crimea?"

"What crime?" he says, not knowing what I was talking about.

"Not crime. Crimea. It's a peninsula in Ukraine. The Russians took it over," I explain.

"Oh, I see. Do we care about it? Do we have to fight the Russians for that?" replies the other guy, obviously more concerned about the fate of the new iPhone than Crimea. He seemed to be asking "for that?" namely for that "little thing"? Is it worth the trouble and expense?

Millions of Americans think like these two college students. And they are not wrong. The United States' isolationism is a topic that has come under discussion many times during the twentieth century. If the United States stays away and doesn't participate in world affairs, is that bad? If it doesn't isolate itself and intervenes to fix the problems, sometimes the outcome is not good—especially when political naïveté gets involved in doomed situations like Vietnam and Iraq.

Perhaps this is what Obama thinks. He's convinced that he was elected (and reelected) because he sees himself as a "transformational" president whose mission is to save the United States from itself: cure capitalism's evils, redress its injustices, and level out its inequalities and discriminations. He is an ideologue—not a politician, like Bill Clinton. Clinton was two notches above Obama because he was able to get both sides to the table to work out compromises.

Sometimes I think that Obama is the American version of Gorbachev. Gorby, a visionary, wanted to reform communism—to make it more bendable and "democratic." He wanted communism with a humane face. But when he got to serious work, the rickety Marxist-Leninist construction—built on dogma, repression, and lies—came down with a thunderous boom. Gorby didn't want to replace the political system inherited from Lenin and Stalin. He only wanted to "improve" it and make it more appealing for the world's downtrodden and the liberal professors at US colleges for whom communism (especially if you live in the West) was not such a bad deal. "No, really"—they seem to think—"There were some bad, freakin' 'apples' like Lenin, Stalin, Mao, Ceausescu, Castro, Pol Pot, Kim-Il-sung, Kim-Jong-il, and others, but the ideology is basically good: equality, fraternity, and no exploitation. It was simply not implemented correctly. Liberty was missing from the equation,[38] and prosperity was just on paper. Other than that, the system was a wonder." I have a question for these professors: why has every Marxist government in history turned repressive? Is it because the ideology itself prioritizes class justice over individual rights and makes no room for diverse opinions? In the United States, a 2011 Rasmussen Reports national survey found that 11 per cent of likely voters think communism is morally superior to the current system of politics and economics. As I and millions of other East Europeans see it, the flops of capitalism are still better than the triumphs of socialism.

Like Gorbachev's communism, Obama thinks that capitalism stinks. It must be reformed, amended, and reorganized. He wants capitalism with a humane face. His only problem is that he is an ideologue. He is inflexible and dogmatic and unable (or unwilling) to reach a compromise with the other side. His plan for a better capitalist society is tax hikes, government handouts, and taking from the rich and giving to the poor: wealth redistribution. (Honestly speaking, this is better than the poverty distribution promoted by communist societies.) What a brilliant idea! To prevent the excesses of capitalism and level out the playing field, his grand plan is to create a large group of people—the so-called "dependents"—who will get a monthly check or other financial assistance to compensate for their meager means of existence. Welfare dependency for the sick and the poor is not a bad idea. But if the able-bodied people prefer to stay home and wait for the welfare check, the society has a problem. Besides, these people will vote for him or his party again in the next elections…and again and again. The problem is, in the United States—unlike in any other Western

---

38 The deadliest ideology in history has claimed an estimated 100 million victims, the vast majority of them in China and the Soviet Union.

country—there are only two parties fighting for temporary dominance. If one of them becomes an eternal winner…what does this smell like? One-party rule? We know pretty well what this means by looking at Eastern Europe after World War II.

If Gorbachev's empire broke up into pieces (Putin is now trying to cobble some of them together), the United States will probably resist the efforts of one person to change the nation's foundational philosophy. Its greatness does not come from its economic might or military prowess. No, it comes from the simple fact that, no matter how dense a US president is, he cannot destroy the nation. There are some good examples to illustrate this. (Bush Jr. was a well-intended simpleton for going to Irak, when the Saddam Hussein dictatorial regime was keeping Iran in check.) Obama is an intelligent president whose true call is academia, not politics. He came with a "vision" and a "plan." It doesn't matter. The country will survive. It is too big to fall. Presidents come and presidents go. Let history take care of them.

I am still disillusioned. The country has changed since I arrived here in 1990. Where is the American exceptionalism, the idea that the United States occupies a special place in the ocean of nations because of the hopes and opportunities it offers for everybody without distinction? You work hard; you can live better. You become a winner. Everybody has the same chance, but you have to be smart and resilient. It seemed as simple as that. Where is the pride to be an American that existed after World War II or when Americans landed on the moon or after the United States won the Cold War? We were so proud of the United States in Eastern Europe and of everything that was American: the free spirit, the economic prowess, the technological and military achievements, the music (we were nuts about Elvis Presley, Mahalia Jackson and Louis Armstrong), the movies, actors, athletes, the freedom of initiative, and even the chewing gum. My friends and I, teenagers at the time, were ecstatic whenever the US athletes beat their Soviet rivals at the Olympic Games. I still remember the names of some of those gold medalists during the '60s: discus thrower Al Oerter, pole vaulter Don Bragg, high jumper John Thomas, sprinter Wilma Rudolph, and many others. We kept statistics on the number of gold and silver medals won by Americans and their chances to finish on top of the Olympic medal table, ahead of the Russians.

Millions of Czechs, Poles, or Romanians were dreaming that one day they'd be able to see the Statue of Liberty at close range. Thousands who were imprisoned for their political views were hoping that the United States would come to rescue them. It was America, Eastern Europe's only hope during its long journey from captivity to liberation, that gave the oppressed people comfort and confidence. There was this kind of idealism or idyllic view of ours. And now it's almost gone. Somebody stole our American dream...

There is an obvious decline in the United States after 2000 precipitated by the terrorist attack on 9/11, the wars in Iraq and Afghanistan, the Great Recession, and Obama's foreign-policy blunders. There have been fourteen years without any major accomplishments under the Bush and Obama administrations, with thousands of Americans killed, many thousands wounded, and trillions of dollars squandered. Now the United States' role and influence in the world is much diminished...dangerously diminished.

"America has become Sissy Nation. A culture of fat, soft, stupid, fearful, whiny, infantile, narcissistic, fatalistic, groupthinking victims. Once we were warriors. Now we're just worriers. Not all Americans are Sissies. But we all swim in the same Sea of Sissiness, and none of us is unaffected by it." [39]

That's how John Strausbaugh describes the United States in his book, *Sissy Nation*. And he goes on:

"Americans used to be known around the world for their pioneering spirit, their bold individualism, their brashness, and ballsiness. We live now in a culture of fear, anxiety, paranoia, and insecurity. We're afraid, literally, of everything. We're afraid of sickness, afraid of death, and afraid to really live. We're afraid of sex. We're afraid

---

39 John Strausbaugh, *Sissy Nation*. (New York: Virgin Books, 2007, 1).

of food. We're afraid of the air, the water, the soil, the weather. We're afraid that the planet itself is rejecting us." [40]

America, shaken by a double crisis of leadership and credibility, is at a crossroads. Europe is at a critical juncture; the whole world is at a turning point. The main issue is not only Russia. Putin, the bare-chested, horse-riding bear hunter, may not be the biggest danger for the world. Russia wants to show that it is a great power—world power, no, regional power, yes. Actually Russia doesn't want to destroy the West because it needs it for its security and prosperity. The Russian economy is tumbling and the poverty rate in the country is rising sharply, thanks to low oil prices and international sanctions. The West and Russia will find a way to work together, eventually—after Putin or Obama—as Russia could also become a major theater for radical Islam.

Can the United States still be considered a beacon of hope and freedom as it was up until 2000? Reagan's America was a shining beacon for those of us living in the unfree Eastern Europe. Do you see Obama saying things like Reagan did at the Berlin Wall: "Mr. Gorbachev, tear down this wall!" No way. He probably thinks that communism was good and noble in its essence (and on paper), only that there were those bloody, rotten "apples": Lenin, Stalin, Mao, Ceausescu, Castro...

These days politicians vow to rid the world of the "bad apples" of Islamic extremism, the "ism" ideology of the twenty-first century. Bin Laden is gone. Other terrorist ideologues are gone. But things are even more complicated and dangerous than before.

America has become a "beacon of freedom" where you have to be careful what you say if you don't want to be labeled a "racist," "extremist," "anti-gay," or "bigot." You are free to be anti-American, anti-Christian, and anti-White, smoke recreational marijuana, and so on. But be careful how you talk about Islam if you don't want to be called an Islamophobe by Obama's ideological zealots.

---

40 Ibidem, 3–4

The presidential elections in 2016 will be a watershed moment—not only for the United States but also for the entire world. We will elect a new US president, and the future of the free world is reliant on it. The drama is that it's hard to see a skilled, honest, nonideological, no double-tongued politician capable of taking the nation from where it is now and leading it successfully to the future.

Hillary Clinton is certain to be the Democrats' presidential nominee if she decides to run for president. For the Republicans, Jeb Bush[41] seems to have a good shot. Thus, for the first time in its history, the United States will set up a nepotistic oligarchy, a battle between the Clintons and the Bushes. I wonder what the Founding Fathers would say. Moreover, these candidates would represent something else: you can only nurture a hope to become president of the United States if you are very rich. If you are middle class or an independent, *adios*. Presidential elections in the United States are a big luxury: each party candidate's expense bill totals at least $1 billion.

Or, perhaps it's time to try something new. Let's pick somebody from outside the political world, somebody who doesn't look and speak like a well rehearsed politician using cheap slogans and making empty promises. Will he (or she) be a better choice?

Like politics, journalism has changed since I came to the United States. The mass media have become acutely partisan; they are at opposite extremes and at loggerheads without moderation. The majority of them, such as newspapers, TV and radio, are machines of polarized propaganda instead of impartial information.

Americans' trust in the media "to report the news fully, accurately and fairly" has dropped to its lowest level in Gallup polling history, with only 32 per cent saying they have a great deal or fair amount of trust in the media.[42] This is down eight percentage points from 2015. Since my arrival

---

41 Jeb Bush, a clunky candidate in a field of more gifted performers, would later drop out of the presidential race.
42 The results of the Gallup survey were published in September 2016, just before I re-published my book.

in 1990 as many as 280 U.S. daily newspapers disappeared, and those that survived saw revenues plummet.

If there ever was a newspaper that one could consider a companion all over the world—from Paris to Hong Kong—it was the Paris-published *International Herald Tribune (IHT)*, a newspaper that became a mainstay of American expatriate culture in Europe after World War I. In October 2013, the *IHT* appeared on newsstands for the last time, being gobbled up by the *New York Times* and renamed the *International New York Times*.

I remember how I used to go to the American Library in Bucharest to read *Newsweek* and the *IHT*. That was the only place in Romania where one could read both publications. I liked the smell of newsprint; I liked the feel of the paper when I opened them and perused them page by page. I felt liberated, and it steeled me to go back to the office where I would have to read *Scanteia (Spark)*, the Communist Party newspaper. The contents were different, and the photos were also different. *Scanteia's* newsprint smelled differently, and the quality of the paper was poor. It was so porous that people used to use it as toilet tissue to save money. And after turning two pages, my fingers would become black from the ink.[43]

The internet, which got the upper hand in the publicity business and has become a free-for-all, signed the death warrant for many newspapers and news people. Technology is a double-edged sword, and the traditional media fell victim to it.

At the AP, the economic crisis and the hasty transition from print to digital, with all its consequences, has led to massive layoffs of reporters and editors—about 10 per cent of payroll. Others were offered incentives to retire, but amazingly, the number of vice presidents stayed the same: about twenty. These days there seem to be more managers than there are reporters, and some of their decisions look bizarre.

Some local overseas offices were temporarily closed, while some bureaus—struggling with a personnel shortage—can hardly meet their

---

43 I recall when I was a kid in the early 1950s there was no toilet paper available, so people had to use scissors to cut scraps of Scanteia and use them as bathroom tissue. Jokes abounded. "Today I rubbed my bottom with [a photo showing] Stalin. And you?" "I did the same with the entire Politburo." There were many variations on this subject.

obligations if a big crisis breaks out in their area. The category of for-eign special correspondents, reporters with special writing skills who roam the world, has disappeared altogether. Now the stories are written fast and with fewer words. Opera, dancing, and Broadway theater re-views, which used to get good play overseas, were discontinued. To free newspersons to do the kind of deeper reporting that only people can do (and to save money on hiring more reporters), AP is now using automa-tion technology to produce business stories about companies earnings reports. Robot writers are replacing human writers. The future starts here. (Japan recently introduced the world's first robotic news anchor that can use a variety of voices and can read the news "without stum-bling once.")

The newsroom in New York, nearly twice as big as a football field, is more than half empty. You look around, and you see desks where no-body works anymore, covered with dust. The computers were removed from many of these desks, and they are left bare and desolate. One of my colleagues looks around at the surrounding emptiness and the deafening silence and comments, "What's this, a mausoleum? A monastery? It's sup-posed to be a newsroom!"

It was until six or seven years ago. My colleagues' morale suffers. Two of them—Pulitzer Prize winners for investigative reporting, Mat Apuzzo and Adam Goldman—said good-bye and joined the *New York Times* and the *Washington Post*. Rukmini Callimachi, born as Maria Sichitiu—the West Africa bureau chief and a Pulitzer Prize finalist—also left for greener pastures. She was the only Romanian employed by the AP, apart from me. And these are just a few examples.

After 2000, the nonprofit Associated Press that for many years had been compared to a family has become like any other company in corpo-rate America: cold and insensitive to its employees' problems. The bottom line, the company's net profit or loss, is what's really important. EBITDA[44]

---

44 EBITDA, a measurement of a company's operating profitability, is Earnings Before Interest, Taxes, Depreciation, and Amortization.

gets more attention than the newsroom workhands—as if the "bottom line" or EBITDA are doing the news reporting and editing.

The executive news editor, a stern person with an air of intense superiority, like an army general, hung a big sign in her office: *No Crabbing*. It's the new media equivalent of "Lasciate ogni speranza, voi ch'entrate" when you go to her office or to human resources (Dante's "Inferno") with a request. (This is valid for all HR offices on the planet). Don't bother her with objections or stupid personal views. Be quiet; be modest. *Do not whine*. (The *No Crabbing* sign reminded me of the *Don't Spit on the Floor* warning in movie theaters in Bucharest after the communist takeover).

I am evaluating my life. Soon I'll retire after forty years of working at AP. For the most part, my colleagues and I were honored to work for a news company that treated its employees with attention and respect. The feelings were mutual. I loved working for AP, which gave me courage and hope when I was in Romania and a steady job in New York. I think I did good in Europe, and when I got into trouble, they came to my aid. I'll ever be grateful for that. Ah, that was the "Old AP"!

The change "from old to new" took place after 2000 when the board of directors, for the first time in more than a hundred years, elected a CEO who didn't come from within the company. (It's a complicated and long story.) After that CEO the next one came from outside too. These people had a different philosophy in dealing with the company's problems and its employees. They had bigger egos and a large gap developed between management and news people, who felt neglected. Disconnected with the newsroom editors and their daily chores, these guys didn't grow with the company, they were parachuted in. It's a shame because the Associated Press is still one of a kind, as it always has been since its creation in 1846. In the ocean of biased and one-sided media in which we drown, AP is the only voice of fair, accurate, nonpartisan, and honest reporting. More than thirty reporters have lost their lives chasing the news in perilous situations since AP's beginning.

Working hard and being responsible, I achieved something. I am the only Romanian who has been employed for such a long time by a Western news medium. And I am the only Romanian who has rubbed elbows in New York for twenty-four years with American reporters and editors who were born in this country.

Together with my wife, I bought a house, I bought and sold five cars through the years, I traveled, and I saw things. I made some money. I am far from being rich, but I am pleased that I don't lack anything now and probably won't in the future.

However, as much as I gained, I lost at the same time. I lost my parents' house in Bucharest where I was born and lived for forty years. I lost my former colleagues and friends in Romania; I have lost contact with most of them. My relationships with some of my family members went cold, for various reasons.

And worst of all, whenever I miss my parents (and I miss them very often), I cannot go to the cemetery and to their graves and thank them for all they did for me. I often tear up when I reflect on my carefree child-hood. They gave my brother and me everything. My biggest regret was to leave my octogenarian father behind when I left Romania; Mom had died several years before.

In each of us there's a winning and a losing side. It's important that the percentage of the winner is at least one per cent more than that of the loser—51–49, at a minimum. Is this what a winner is?

I left my native country for various reasons—abandoning everything I had there, coming, working, and living as an immigrant in the world at large. Life is an adventure, even if you are not an adventurer. I can't complain about my achievements. Things went well. But everything is a zero-sum game. What you earn in apples, you lose in pears, as a Romanian saying goes. I move back and forth because I live in two worlds: the United States, which has meant so much for me and millions like me, and Romania, where I have my roots and tons of memories.

I wish that things were good *here* where I live and *there* where I was born. But this is not happening.

So how do you feel when the world around you is struggling with all kinds of problems that it created and is not capable of solving? How do you feel when the incompetent and hypocritical politicians we elect are steal-ing the future of our children?

You feel … take your pick: troubled, bubbled, crumbled, fumbled, humbled, jumbled, stumbled, tumbled, juggled, struggled, booed, skewed, stewed, screwed …

Chorus:

*It's a world of laughter*
*A world of tears.*
*It's a world of hopes*
*And a world of fears…*

# Swan Song

On my last work day I sent my colleagues this final e-mail:

Dear colleagues and friends,

After 40 years and 8 1/2 months, I have reached the end of my journey as a journalist. And what a journey it was! From the Siberia of freezing apartments, food shortages and political repression (that was Ceausescu's Romania) to the Cyberia of cyber snooping, American "unexceptionalism" and political correctness (which is Obama's America). In between the two worlds, I spent three years in the schnitzel-loving Vienna covering the anti-communist revolutions in the former Soviet bloc together with my colleagues there.

Here is my self-evaluation for my HR file:
Full name: SERGIU VIOREL URMA
IN: September 1973
OUT: May 2014

1.  In a few words, explain what your physical/mental condition is.

Not only don't I have any preexisting conditions, I don't even have an existing condition, to the desperation of my PCP whom I see only once or twice a year. Neither communism or capitalism, nor 40 years with the AP, could do any harm or damage to my system.

Rating scale: well above expectations.

2.  Name a successful project that you were involved in.

I am the creator of GP (not Grand Prix, but G Priority, with "g" as in gravity) - the lowest level of urgency and visibility for a story to move. It applies to those stories for which there's no huge international interest. While they may be newsworthy for the national U.S. market, for global consumption they are not, therefore instead of hitting and clogging the world wires, these stories, obeying the basic law of physics, are pulled down by the force of gravity and hit the ground (waste paper basket) in New York.

Rating scale: above expectations.

3.  Name one thing that you don't regret.

Working for AP, the only news medium that delivers unbiased news and unfiltered information. In this regard, it is unique. As politicians and governments screw up and suck all over the world, and "work" hard to tell their side of the story or cover up their mess, it never was as difficult and risky to be objective, keep a cool head and report things truthfully as it is today, and AP strives to fulfill its historic mission, oftentimes under adverse conditions. My hope is that it will afford to remain independent in the future, as it is today. As somebody who knows firsthand what totalitarian censorship is and how it works, I'd like to say this: freedom of speech - and an independent press - is not something that falls from the sky. If you don't have it, you have to fight for it; and you if are lucky to have it, you must defend it at all costs. (By the way, political correctness in Eastern Europe was called self-censorship. Zip up your mouths, comrades!) For many years, while I was reporting from Romania, AP was my umbilical cord to the free world. It offered me courage and hope, and it gave a new meaning to my life, for which I am immensely thankful. I was a prisoner like the other 23 million Romanians, but despite threats over the telephone from "anonymous" callers, I felt like I was "free." The AP teleprinter in the Bucharest office gave me that feeling and made all the difference.

Rating scale: above expectations.

4.  Name one thing that you regret.

The only time I was allowed to travel to the West by the communist authorities (before I had to leave the country for good), I toured the AP bureaus in Frankfurt and Vienna. Across the street from our bureau in Frankfurt, I noticed a big sign: Dr. Muller's Sex World. As curious as somebody who is released from prison and stops at the first bordello on his way home, I sprinted to see the first porno movie in my life. I paid the equivalent of $10 for a ticket, which included a little box of Swiss chocolates. The show started and after some 15 minutes two guys seated several rows behind me started hyperventilating while strange noises and moans came from a corner of the hall. All of a sudden, I realized that I was sitting in the crossfire of action: there was "action" on the screen and "action" in the theater, something that I did not expect. I thought that Dr. Muller's movie-goers would be as disciplined as the masses seeing communist-sanctioned films behind the Iron Curtain. But they were not. As the moans got closer and more intense, I said to myself: "Geez, I'd better get the fuck out of here. It's more dangerous than reporting from Romania," and I left. I was disappointed and I felt guilty for spending $10 for a tiny box of chocolates. The next day, from the generous per diem allowance approved by New York (the year was 1980, the "old" AP) I bought my wife two skirts and two blouses. As far as I know, Dr. Muller's is still in business today, an illustration of the robustness of the German economy in a time of crisis.

Rating scale: much below expectations.

5.   Elaborate on a few things you intend to improve.

Working on a book for a Romanian publisher, trading stocks from my home computer, playing the piano (mostly Scarlatti, Bach and Argentine tangos), going more often to the Met (opera and museum), visiting the Hudson Valley wineries (as part of my personal Wellness program), etc.

Rating scale: meets expectations.

6.   Where do you see yourself 50 years from now?

It depends. If there'll be no company pension and Social Security benefits left in place I'll have to move back to my native Romania, if the country won't become part of Greater Russia, which in its turn might be swallowed by Greater China.

Rating scale: much below expectations.

7.   Elaborate on media problems today, as you see them, in 300 words.

There is a striking similarity between modern journalism and classical music. Take Richie Wagner (VAGH-nur) and the Wagner Festival at Bayreuth (not to be confused with Beirut). *Tristan und Isolde* lasts five hours; *Goetterdaemmerung* is even worse, six hours, from 6 p.m. to midnight. Who, *mein lieber Schatz*, has the patience to spend six hours of his life listening to VAGH-nur, when you can sit in the comfort of your home and listen to Lady Gaga? So what can you do to save money? Cut the fat! Competition is fierce and resources are tight. Listeners, like readers, have a short span of attention. Beautiful music is like beautiful writing: boring. Make it simple, keep it short. Let's face it: even Dick Vagner (sp?) needs a manager to teach him how to trim stuff and cut costs. Cut the string instruments of the orchestra by 20 percent. Fiddlers are like news clerks (aka editorial assistants): a waste of money! Make *Tristan* last only three hours. Trim the lyrics of Isolde's *Liebestod* aria in Act 3 to only 300 words. Who needs so much music and so many words? Didn't they blame Mozart for writing "too many notes"? (These days nobody reads a 300-plus-word story unless it's about a terrorist attack or the Kardashians) And if you are a music manager and you really want to impress your HR folks in New York, trim it further to just 100 words. On the extra-plus side, because there are fewer words, the soprano can remember the lyrics and won't need a prompter ... so cut that position and here you are! You get a bonus or a promotion. And please stop producing opera reviews. Nobody reads them in Albany ... or is it Albania? Never mind. Justin Bieber sells better, from Maldives to Moldova. The bottom line: smaller orchestras and newsrooms. Fewer notes and fewer words (except in TV talk shows and the blogosphere, blah blah), if you can still believe them. Quality journalism is hard to come by these days. Crappy times.

Rating scale: meets the lowest expectations.

8. Elaborate on what type of work you see yourself doing in the near future.

I'd better let Hemingway speak for myself. I have a deep respect and admiration for him, for being able to create in simple words and short sentences so much substance and render such rich meanings behind the uncomplicated text that nobody else could match him. He started as a newspaper reporter, long before the internet messed up everything. His direct, factual, unadorned prose writing style owed so much to his work as a journalist.

This is what he said in a *Paris Review* interview in 1958:

"The most essential gift for a good writer is a built-in, shock-proof, shit detector. This is the writer's radar …"

If I were to start a private business, I'd like to pursue a career in the manufacturing of "built-in, shock-proof, shit detectors" to be used by government spin masters, political commentators and politicians the world over. I could strike it rich and famous that only in America one can become. And for a very good cause.

For Hemingway was a genius.

Cheers and good luck!

# Postscript

I am still waiting for the National Council for the Study of the Securitate Archives to tell me the actual names of Securitate's sources—"Cornel," "Andrei," "Tudora," "Horia," "Corina," "Petre," "Coman," "Costin," and "Armasu"—mentioned in my dossier, as I was promised. Could it be that these agents were from my circle of friends or perhaps neighbors? I am very curious because I picked my friends and acquaintances with great care. It would devastate me if any of those spying on me were from my own family.

## About the Author

Sergiu Viorel Urma was an AP reporter and editor for forty years. He worked in Bucharest, Romania, where he was born, in Vienna, Austria, and in New York City. He is a graduate of the University of Bucharest and holds a master's degree in English Language and Literature. His memoir, *Screwed: Dancing with the Generals*, is his first book. His two-act play, *Chessgame*, was published by *Modern International Drama*, a magazine of contemporary, international drama in translation, published by the State University of New York at Binghamton in 1996. He lives with his wife and son in New Jersey.

CPSIA information can be obtained
at www.ICGtesting.com
Printed in the USA
LVHW081601120819
627339LV00035B/1702/P

9 780692 413500